The Story of Yogi Berra

(Wide World Photos)

Gene Schoor

The Story of Yogi Berra

DOUBLEDAY & COMPANY, INC.
GARDEN CITY, NEW YORK   1976

Library of Congress Cataloging in Publication Data

Schoor, Gene.
The story of Yogi Berra.

Includes index.
SUMMARY: A biography of Yogi Berra, who spent most
of his baseball career behind home plate for the New
York Yankees.
1. Berra, Yogi, 1925–   —Juvenile literature.
2. Baseball—Juvenile literature. [1. Berra, Yogi,
1925–   2. Baseball—Biography] I. Title.
GV865.B4S36   796.357′092′4 [B] [92]
Library of Congress Catalog Card Number 76–2823
ISBN: 0-385-11020-0 Trade
0-385-11021-9 Prebound

Chapter 1

It was the summer of 1941. In Europe, Hitler's armies had already occupied most of France and were invading Russia. The Japanese attack on Pearl Harbor was but a few months off.

But it was neither Hitler nor the war that was uppermost in the minds of the two youngsters who approached Sportsman's Park, home of the St. Louis Cardinals, this summer of 1941. It was baseball and the glories of the game that occupied them completely. The two young men in question were not interested in just watching their big league heroes make those fantastic catches in the field, or hammer the ball out of the park. Nor was it one of those crucial games between the Cards and the Dodgers, the Giants, or the Cubs, that they were set to witness.

It was an occasion that was more important than that, more important than anything that either of them had experienced in their young lives. They were walking into Sportsman's Park to show the officials of the Cardinal club what they could do with the bat, with the glove, with the ball. They were going to demon-

1

strate to the coaches that here were two young fellows the St. Louis organization should sign to a big league contract. They were here, these two young boys, at the invitation of the club, to try out for the team.

"Don't be nervous."

"Who's nervous?"

Everybody who has ever had a baseball glove on his hand, swung a bat, fielded a hot smash to third, or caught a fly ball has dreamed of glories on the diamond, has pictured himself making that heroic, tumbling, shoestring catch of a sinking liner to save the game in the ninth inning, has had visions of himself rocketing that mighty four-base wallop, clearing the fences, clearing the bases with that dramatic come-from-behind four-run homer to put the game on the winning side of the ledger for the home team. And no one in the United States was more imbued with such dreams than the two youngsters who briskly opened the doors into Sportsman's Park and entered the Cardinal's dressing room.

One was Joe Garagiola. The other had been christened Lawrence Peter Berra. Both youngsters had starred for the St. Louis American Legion Stockham Post. They were both essentially catchers. Each had his own sponsor. The Cardinal scout Dee Walsh, whose job it was to find talent for the club in the St. Louis area was sponsoring Garagiola. Jack Maguire, another Cardinal scout, was proposing Berra. Recommendation by a scout, however, did not guarantee a contract with a baseball club. The manager of the team—and particularly the front office of the organization—had to be convinced.

"Did you bring your lunch?"

"You know I brought my lunch."

"A banana hero sandwich?"

"With mustard."

"Ugh! How can you eat it?"

"With my teeth."

Maybe his banana hero sandwiches, with mustard, made everybody else sick, but it was Berra's favorite lunch. He wasn't going to change his routine, not this day of all days. Sudden changes in routines bring sudden changes in luck. It wasn't that the young fellow was superstitious, but he wasn't taking any chances.

"You'll starve to death on those skinny little sandwiches in that bag of yours," he said.

If anything, young Berra was a bit more relaxed than his pal, Joe Garagiola. He was the better ballplayer of the two, and both boys knew it, though Garagiola looked more the part of a professional athlete.

Actually, Berra looked like anything but an athlete. He might have passed easily enough for a wrestler, or even a weight lifter; but as a ballplayer, even a sandlot ballplayer? No.

He was a heavy-set young fellow. He was squat. His short legs made him look even shorter than he really was.

"He's built like a fire hydrant," said his friends.

They said a lot worse of him, and they would continue to say a lot worse of him in the days to come, and not behind his back either. It wasn't that he wasn't well-liked. Joe Garagiola, his pal for life, worshiped him. But Berra just lent himself to the kind of cruelty young boys inflict on each other. He took everything as it came. He never scowled, never retaliated. He would just smile or, at worst, pay no attention to the jibe; and the jibes came fast and furiously.

His best friends made fun of his looks (he was not the handsomest man in the world). They laughed at the way he stuck his nose into comic books. They howled at the way he butchered the English language.

"You're a regular yogi!"

The boys had just come out of a movie theater where they had seen some B picture set in India.

"Just look at him!"

It was Jack Maguire, son of the Cardinal scout, and later a regular with the New York Giants.

"He looks like a yogi. He walks like a yogi. Yogi!"

"Yogi!"

"Yogi!"

The name stuck.

It was no longer Lawrence, or Larry as the boys called him, or Lawdie as his mother called him. It was Yogi.

"Hey, Yogi! Come on, Yogi!"

For a while young Berra tried to avoid the nickname. For a while, until some clubhouse general corrected the situation, he even autographed baseballs "Lawrence Peter Berra."

"Who's Lawrence Peter?" demanded the clubhouse guard. "The only Berra the fans know is Yogi!"

Yogi it was, and Yogi it stayed.

No one is insensitive to ugly remarks, and young Yogi Berra was as sensitive as anyone else, maybe more sensitive, to the unflattering comment, the mean word, the foul gesture. What he did about it, however, is what just most people can't. He put all that unpleasant name calling, and all the other unpleasantries he was forced to confront, into a proper perspective. What really mattered to Yogi was baseball. This he knew from the beginning, and he didn't have to go to school to learn it. The ball game was the thing and nothing else really counted. So long as he could play the game like a professional, hammer the ball better than anyone else around him, then all was right with the world for Yogi Berra. No one loved baseball better than Yogi. It was his entire life.

"The Ape" is what Bucky Harris, the boy-wonder manager who led the Washington Senators to a World Championship in 1924, called him. Bucky would later manage the Yankees and Yogi.

In the summer of 1941 he knew he was the best ballplayer on the St. Louis American Legion Stockham Post nine, and he was certain that he'd have no difficulty impressing the Cardinal coaches with his baseball prowess.

Fortunately, at the time, Yogi did not know that Sportman's Park was not the scene of his first tryout for a major league baseball career. He did not even know that he had had a previous tryout. He might have been a little less confident if he had known, and one needs all the confidence one can muster for these tryouts. He might have also been a little better prepared for the suffering he would experience at the end of that summer day.

Leo Browne, the American Legion post commander, had recognized the tremendous potential in young Berra, and he had urged the sportswriter for the St. Louis Globe-Democrat, Bob Burnes, to take a look at him in action.

"You may think he's a bit clumsy," said Leo

5

Browne, "but there isn't a position on the diamond he can't play. He can even pitch, if he has to. He isn't one of your long-legged sprinters, but he can move around those bases fast. And he can hit! He'll take a bad swing once in a while, like any other inexperienced player, but he'll wallop anything that comes near the plate. And he'll wallop it for a mile. He has the fastest wrists I've ever seen."

Bob Burnes went to see Yogi perform one day. He had looked at maybe a hundred youngsters touted by a hundred fans. Baseball greats come from the oddest places in the smallest towns of these widespread United States. No one knows for sure that he won't be missing up on a potential great ballplayer, if he neglects some obscure game in some obscure sand lot of some obscure town. Burnes wasn't going to let this opportunity of witnessing a future star go by, particularly since he had much respect for the baseball judgment of his friend Leo Browne.

Burnes watched Yogi. This was a day when Yogi was playing third base, not his best position, and Bob Burnes was not overly impressed with his play. He saw Yogi swing at a low inside pitch and hit the ball clear over the fence, and this made Burnes sit up and take notice. But he also saw the young ballplayer swing at a pitch that was over his head, and go down on strikes; he was not impressive at third base and let a base hit bounce off his chest for an error. "I think you're oversold on him," said the sportswriter to Leo Browne, and the post commander could say nothing. Yogi Berra's first tryout for a possible major league contract was over and done with. It was a story Yogi was to hear years later, and from Bob Burnes himself.

In Sportsman's Park, this summer of 1941, Yogi was making a desperate try for a chance to play professional ball and make a career of it.

He glanced up into the shade of the stands where he knew that Branch Rickey was sitting. Branch Rickey was the general manager of the St. Louis club and already a legend in baseball. He looked out on to the field where his pal Joe Garagiola was showing his stuff to the all-powerful Cardinal coaches, the men who would either provide or deny that so-urgently desired contract, the contract that would spell the beginning of a dream come true, life as a big league professional baseball star.

Garagiola was graceful behind the plate. He quickly scooped up a bunt and snapped it accurately to the first baseman. He ran the bases swiftly. He hit the ball hard. He was fluid and his actions were flawless.

Yogi tried to concentrate. He knew he could get that bunt as fast as Joe Garagiola, maybe faster, but he knew, too, that he was not as graceful as Joe. Nor could he run the bases as gracefully as Joe. But he could hit! Joe Garagiola reached the fence with a clout of his bat. Yogi determined to clear that fence. He did.

Yogi knew his weaknesses. He knew he was awkward and clumsy behind the plate. He knew that he took his catching position too far behind the hitter. He was aware that base runners were stealing on him; but he had hit the ball solidly. That's what counts in baseball . . . solid base hits. He felt sure that he had accomplished what he intended; to impress the top scouts and Branch Rickey of the St. Louis Cardinals. And when an overjoyed Joe Garagiola emerged from

7

the inner offices of the Cardinals, to announce that he not only had won a contract, but a $500 bonus as well, Yogi was certain that his own professional career was about to begin. He was to be bitterly disappointed.

As a matter of fact, Branch Rickey didn't even bother to invite Yogi into his office. For all purposes, Yogi did not impress Rickey and was not offered a contract.

It was one of the biggest disappointments of his life.

Yogi was utterly bewildered. He couldn't understand the situation at all. He was a better ballplayer than Garagiola—they all knew it, but not Branch Rickey.

"I don't understand it," said Yogi.

"Neither do I," said the Cardinal scout, Jack Maguire.

He went in to see Rickey.

"We can't let this boy go," he argued.

"Why?" asked Rickey. "He's clumsy. He's slow. Can't throw. Maybe he'll make Triple-A ball, but that's all. I want boys who will make it all the way. We need youngsters who can run like a deer, with great throwing arms. This boy, Berra, is slow, awkward."

Maguire insisted that Rickey wasn't making a wise judgment.

"He's young. Has great potential," he persisted.

"Triple-A," repeated Branch Rickey. "You can offer him $250 to sign up. That's all he's worth. And I'm not sure he's worth that."

Maguire brought the offer to Yogi, and Yogi shook his head in disbelief.

"If Joey Garagiola is worth $500, so am I."

They could tag him with funny names, they could poke fun at his face, they could laugh at him all they wanted to, but they could not belittle his baseball ability. He was the best American Legion ballplayer in St. Louis, and he was proud of it. No one, but no one —not even Branch Rickey—was going to downgrade him where it came to playing the game.

Yogi was hurt. Hurt deeply. He was happy for his pal Joey, but the disappointment he suffered in Sportsman's Park that summer afternoon was a cruel blow to young Yogi Berra.

It was rumored in later years that Branch Rickey, who was moving over to the Brooklyn Dodger organization the next year, wanted to keep Berra out of the public eye so that he could sign him for the Brooklyn club at a later time. To this day, Yogi, along with most of the sports world, won't believe that Branch Rickey was playing it that way. Rickey was too honest a man for that kind of dealing. What happened in Sportsman's Park was simply that Rickey made a mistake. General managers, as well as managers and scouts, are not free from errors in judgment when it comes to seeing the potential of a young and still far-from-tried young ballplayer.

Jack Maguire had too much faith in Yogi's ability to forget his young protégé by listening to Rickey's curt dismissal. He talked to Lou McQuillen, who was a scout for the St. Louis American League ball club, the Browns.

"I don't see why Rickey turned him down," he said. "He's got the makings of a great ballplayer, and you can sign him up for just a $500 bonus."

McQuillen took the message and the recom-

9

mendation to his front office, but he had no more luck than Maguire had with Rickey.

"We'll sign him up, if you think he's that good," they said, "but no bonus."

"No bonus, no contract," said Berra. "I want what Joey got, $500, or I don't play."

A sense of his own values, a knowledge of his own abilities, as well as pride, were all that were left to the young Yogi Berra. But pride and the knowledge of his own worth were of little consolation, at that time anyway, to a deeply depressed young man. Nor could he have possibly guessed, for all his disappointment, for all of his depression, that the failures of both St. Louis clubs to offer him that measly $500 were to lead to the happy beginning of one of the greatest careers in the history of baseball.

Chapter 2

Pietro Berra was a tenant farmer in Malvaglio in the northern part of Italy near the big city of Milan. Like so many other Italians in the early 1900s, he left his native land for the hope and the promise of a better life in America. He moved West, to California, where he got a job as a farmhand.

The idea that weighed most on his mind was to save up enough money to bring his Italian sweetheart, Paulina, across the Atlantic to join him in the States, but the California job didn't pay enough to make that dream possible. He moved on to Colorado, where he worked in a construction gang. He wasn't afraid of work, but his savings didn't amount to much. Pietro was on the move again. This time he got a job as a bricklayer, working on the St. Louis Arena; and finally he landed work with Laclede-Christy, the St. Louis brickmakers.

St. Louis became his home. He sent for Paulina, who had been waiting for him in Malvaglio, they were married in St. Ambrose Church and settled down in the Hill section—the Little Italy of St. Louis—to raise their family. This was in 1911, just three years before the whole continent of Europe (and later the United States) became involved in the First World War.

There were five children born to the Berras. First there was Anthony, then Michael, then John. The fourth was christened Lawrence Peter. His mother, who never learned to speak English, called him Lawdie. The fifth child was a girl, the only girl in the family, Angelina.

Pietro ruled his little family with an iron hand. He was the old-fashioned Italian father. No one could have loved his children more, but he insisted on the kind of discipline he had learned and lived under in the old country. No one could say "No" to Papa. His word was law and, often enough, he enforced that law with his good, strong right hand. Mamma was more gentle. She never whipped the boys. But, except for the very rare occasion, she saw to it that Papa administered whatever punishment he deemed necessary for any infraction of the family code of behavior.

It was Papa's "old-fashioned" idea that a man must work. He could not understand the American love for sports. He frowned on sports as a waste of time. All the Berra boys were naturally gifted ballplayers, but Papa Pietro would have none of it in his family, and with the exception of Yogi, Papa had his way.

Anthony was a fine fielder and a good hitter, and the Cleveland Indians invited him to try out for a place in their organization. Papa said, "No!" And "No" it was.

Michael actually did try out for the St. Louis Browns and was offered a minor league contract.

Again Papa said, "No!"

12

Ballplaying was for boys, as Papa Pietro Berra saw it. Men must work.

Anthony, or "Lefty" as he was called, was the best ballplayer in the family, according to Yogi, but it was Yogi alone, after some considerable struggle and not without a series of family crises, who broke down his father's resistance to the game of baseball as a man's career.

Yogi began to play ball when he was old enough to hold a bat and swing at a ball on the lot at the end of Elizabeth Street, in the Hill section of St. Louis of course. When he was about eleven years old, the kids of the neighborhood organized themselves into a sports club, which they called the Stags A. C. With hand-me-down gloves, splintered bats, and well-worn base-balls, they played in the streets, or in the schoolyards, sometimes in nearby Sublette Park.

Finding a place to play baseball within the city limits was no easy task even in those days, but the Stags A. C. managed. They even turned a garbage dump into a baseball diamond. They found two old wrecks of cars and dragged them into position to serve as two dugouts for the opposing teams. The baseball enthusiasm of the young fellows on the Hill overcame all obstacles; except one. Papa Pietro Berra remained adamant in his opposition to anything resembling sports competition.

"You didn't get all that dirt on your face working!" Smack! "You tore your pants again!" Smack! "When are you going to grow up and be like a man?" Smack!

"Hey, Mom!" young Berra would call from outside the door to the house. "Is Pop home?"

If Papa were home, there would be no escaping that

good right-hand wallop. If he weren't, maybe Mamma would be kind this time and forget to tell Papa that young Lawdie had ripped the knees of his pants just one more time, sliding into third base, taking a fall in soccer, or being tackled in some tough scrimmage in football.

Yogi played in all of the games, and hard. He was a good soccer player. He was a fierce charging back in football, a better-than-average basketball player, and a considerably better-than-average competitor in the boxing ring. He was even a good man to have on your side in a hockey game.

Actually Yogi had some ten fights as a semiprofessional. That is, the fights were billed as amateur, but Yogi got five or ten dollars, depending on the gate at the Italian-American Club, for each night's work in the ring. He had his first fight when he was only fourteen years old, and he won it. He won seven of the next eight, and came back to avenge his lone defeat with much dash and vigor in his tenth fight. Incidentally, all the money he earned fighting went to Mamma. As a matter of fact, everything Yogi earned for a good many years went to Mamma. That's the way things were done in a strict Italian-American family. The young fellows turned in their pay checks to Mamma, no matter how much they were, and Mamma would dole out two or three dollars, depending on the money earned, as spending money.

Yogi's only interest in money those days was to earn enough so that Mamma would give him money to buy himself a new baseball glove, spiked shoes, maybe a catcher's mask and, some day, a baseball uniform, the kind the rich kids wore.

14

At this time, if you were a member of the Cardinals' Knothole Gang, you could see the Cardinals play ball every Saturday they were at home, free of charge; and Yogi Berra was a member of the Cardinals' Knothole Gang, sponsored by a kind lady who lived across the street, a Miss Beltrami. Yogi would never forget. Frankie Frisch, the Fordham Flash; Dizz Dean; Paul Dean; Joe ("Ducky") Medwick; Wild Bill Hallahan; Leo ("The Lip") Durocher; Frank Orsatti; Pepper Martin; these were the stars of the St. Louis Club when Yogi was a boy, these were the men Yogi, sitting away up in the left-field stands, idolized.

"One of these days," he dreamed, and his days were filled with imaginary heroics on the diamond, the impossible catch, the grand-slam winning home run.

The first organized league Yogi played in was in a league created by Joe Causino, secretary of the local Y.M.C.A. It was a league whose ball clubs were sponsored by local shops and merchants who provided their boys with their uniforms and other baseball equipment. The only nine that wasn't sponsored was the Stags A. C., Yogi's club, and they didn't have any uniforms either. The Stags came from the Hill, and Italian shopkeepers didn't think much of baseball.

"Soccer? Yes. That's a man's game!"

"Baseball? Phew! That's a bum's game!"

The Stags had no uniforms. As a matter of fact, they didn't have enough baseball gloves to go around. But they did pretty well in that league, coming in second only to Edmonds of the Recreation Intermediate League.

It was the Edmonds team that lured both Yogi and Joe Garagiola from the Stags, who were breaking up

15

anyway, and it was for the Edmonds that Yogi Berra wore his first baseball suit. It was one of the proudest days in his life when he first suited up in the Edmond uniform. He and Joey looked at each other and then gravely shook hands. "Now we look like real players," said Yogi.

But there was always Papa, Pietro Berra. Papa's shift at the Laclede-Christy brickworks was over at four-thirty, and Yogi's job was to have his pitcher of beer on the table by the time Papa got home. That meant Yogi had to get home from wherever he was—usually on some ball field—get the fifteen cents for the beer from Mamma, run to the saloon to get the pitcher filled, and run all the way back home before Papa arrived.

"Cold enough, Pop?"

"Cold enough."

If the beer wasn't there on the table, Yogi would be in trouble, and he knew it. It was no unusual sight to see young Berra drop his bat in a crucial inning and make tracks, once that Laclede-Christy quitting time whistle began to blow. And young Joey Garagiola, whose father worked alongside of Pietro Berra, would also always be running on that urgent errand, along with Yogi, and for the same reason.

But Joey Garagiola had one advantage over his pal Yogi. Joey had no difficulty with his schoolwork. Yogi just couldn't study. Joey went on to high school after graduating from the local elementary school. Yogi got out of the elementary school with the help of some kind teachers, and that was the end of his formal education.

Papa Berra invited the principal of the school and

the priest of the parish to his house to discuss the educational problems of young Yogi.

"I don't want my son to become a bum. I want him to continue in school!"

Papa and Mamma were worried. The principal and the parish priest were kind.

"It is sometimes better for a young man to go to work. Not everybody is born a scholar."

Yogi was no scholar. He went to work.

His first job was with a coal company. He didn't like it. He hated it. He hated being dirty all the time. Worse, he hated working in the afternoons, knowing that Joey Garagiola and all the other fellows who went on to high school were playing ball. Yogi began to disappear from the coal yards, calling it a day by three o'clock.

"Where were you yesterday afternoon?"

"I didn't feel good."

"You don't feel good every afternoon."

"Not every afternoon."

"Well, you can take this afternoon off, and tomorrow morning, and the day after. We don't need you here."

He got other jobs, but the lure of the baseball fields made every job he had untenable. There were no jobs that ended at three o'clock, time for baseball practice or the game, and the game was more important than anything else to Yogi. He had even begun to dare the wrath of his father because of this love for the baseball diamond.

"You were making good money," said Papa Berra.

He had earned twenty-five dollars a week, working in the coal-yard. He had earned twenty-seven dollars a week, working on a soft drink truck. That was a lot of money for a young fellow in those days. He wasn't interested in girls, an interest that might have necessitated a larger allowance from Mamma and perhaps a steady job. As a matter of fact, Yogi was so afraid of girls, he would walk across the street to avoid meeting a girl he had known in school. He didn't need money for girls. He could live without money if only he was allowed to play ball.

"Ball! Ball! That's all you think about! What's going to become of you? A bum? A bum?"

Bum defined a number of conditions in the Berra household: a loafer, an idler, someone who was bound to get into trouble. Yogi wasn't thinking along the lines of his father.

"I want to become a professional ballplayer."

"That's a bum!" exploded Papa Berra. "My son wants to become a bum! What have I done to deserve this thing in my own family?"

In desperation, Papa Berra called another family meeting. Anthony and Michael were invited, with, of course, Mamma. The whole family, including the brothers, was down on Yogi by this time. The priest of the parish of St. Ambrose, Father Koester, was also asked to attend the family crisis get-together, as was Joe Causino, the secretary of the local Y.M.C.A.

Papa Berra, in the presence of the esteemed Y.M.C.A. secretary and the parish priest, was restrained. He simply stated the case against his son.

"A man should work," he said. "I am afraid that what my son is doing is no good for him, no good for his family. The truth is that I am afraid he will become bad."

Father Koester was deliberate, gentle, but firm.

"There is nothing wrong with playing baseball," he said. "Baseball is a good thing, but it is not everything. I think your mother and father are not wrong to be worried about you. You can play baseball, but there are other things in life and you have to attend to those things, too."

Yogi may not have been the best student when it came to academic subjects, but he always had, from his earliest days, a sharp understanding of human beings, their thinking, and their emotions. He knew that the only person in the room he might enlist to his cause was Joe Causino, the man from the Y, the man who had always been a friend to the kids in the Hill section.

"You told us a man ought to spend his life doing what interested him," said Yogi to the Y secretary.

"That's right," said Joe Causino. "That's what we're trying to tell you. You've got to make up your mind about that interest and give it all you've got."

"Yeah," said Yogi.

"Well, what's it going to be, Larry?" pressed Joe Causino.

Yogi looked at him for a moment, looked at everyone else in the room.

"Baseball," he said. "That's what it's got to be. Baseball."

Papa Berra jumped from his chair. If Joe Causino and Father Koester hadn't been there, he would have knocked Yogi clean across the room.

The good Father restrained him.

"Not everyone who wants to play baseball can make a profession of it."

19

"I can make it."

"And suppose you don't?"

"I want the chance."

"You owe something to your family. These are hard times."

"I'll sell newspapers at night. I'll get odd jobs. I'll do my share."

"I think," said Father Koester to Papa Berra, "that we ought to let Larry try, give him a reasonable amount of time to try.

"If you can't make it, Larry," he said, turning to the young Berra, "then I think we can expect you to try to do something that is not baseball."

It was a deal that left nobody in the room but Yogi happy. Papa, Mamma, even his two brothers were skeptical about the whole business, for different reasons. Papa and Mamma didn't look on baseball as work, let alone a career. His brothers, Anthony and Michael, knew how tough it was to get into the big leagues, to make baseball really pay off.

But young Yogi was all smiles. For the first time in his life no one at home was going to hassle him about his playing ball. For once he didn't have to take on a job that would keep him out of the game. At last he was free to play ball wherever and whenever he wanted. And he did not doubt for a moment that he would ever have to quit playing ball, that baseball was to be not only his career but his life.

"What's it going to be?" Joe Causino had asked.

"Baseball," said Yogi. "That's what it's got to be. Baseball."

Chapter 3

In the last years of the great depression, which began in 1929 with the stock market crash, the W.P.A. (the Works Progress Administration) organized a baseball school for the young boys of St. Louis. The school was held regularly in one of St. Louis' public playgrounds, Sherman Park, and Enos Slaughter and Terry Moore, two of the St. Louis Cardinals stars, were among the ballplayers who appeared on a somewhat regular basis to teach the boys the finer points of the game.

Yogi, as well as Joey Garagiola, never missed a session. Just being near the two great St. Louis outfielders made their hearts beat a bit faster. More important, maybe Yogi wasn't very quick learning things out of a book, but he was quick enough to learn everything the professional ballplayers were there to teach him. He learned many of the finer points of the game while playing with the American Legion Stockham post, a good amateur team that made it to the semifinals of the American Legion tournament twice. Then came Yogi's tryout, which was a complete failure. The failure hit Yogi hard.

"They can say anything they want to say about my looks, about what I eat, about the way I talk, but no one can say I'm not a good ballplayer."

There was no doubt that he had been deeply hurt, that his pride had been stepped on and mauled, but for all the depression that followed the Sportsman's Park episode, Yogi lost none of his self-confidence. He knew he had the ability to be a real ballplayer, and no one could take that away from him.

Yogi had promised that he would give up the game and go to work if he could not make good in baseball. To all appearances, he had failed in his very first effort to make a good showing in the St. Louis tryouts. How could he explain that Joey Garagiola had received a $500 bonus while all that was offered him, and only after some extra effort by Jack Maguire, was $250?

He didn't try to explain. Papa Berra wouldn't have understood anyway. Yogi went back to work.

He took a job with the Johansen's Shoe Company. He was a tack puller on ladies' shoes, and the more tacks he pulled the more money he earned. He wasn't bad at it and was soon earning as much as forty-five dollars a week. The money was of considerable help to the Berra family, and Mamma and Papa were quite pleased to see their son doing something they considered a good deal more significant than playing baseball. Mamma even raised his allowance to three dollars a week.

But Yogi did not forget baseball. He managed to get into uniform with several semiprofessional ball clubs, played nights and weekends, for five and ten dollars a game. It wasn't much, and it certainly wasn't what he had dreamed of as the goal for his baseball career. But better times, happily, for Yogi and the baseball world were on their way.

Maybe Branch Rickey gave up quickly on the potential of Yogi Berra as a ballplayer, but there were others in St. Louis who hadn't. One of those people who saw the future in Yogi's glove and Yogi's bat was Leo Browne.

Leo Browne was head of the American Legion program in St. Louis. He had been an umpire at one time in the Eastern Baseball League when George Weiss managed the New Haven club. George Weiss was now the general manager of the New York Yankees, and Leo Browne wrote him a letter. He didn't pull any punches in the letter. He told Weiss everything he had told sportswriter Bob Burnes before.

"His form is terrible, but he can sock that ball a mile. He looks clumsy, but he's not. Everything he does seems to be wrong, but it comes out fine. He'll sign up for any kind of contract you offer him, but he has to have a $500 bonus. That's the kind of kid he is."

Weiss respected the opinion of Leo Browne, but he wanted to check on it.

"Leo Browne," he said to his bull-pen coach, Johnny Schulte, "says he has a kid worth looking at. Check on him. See what he can do. Sign him up, if you like what you see, and if it doesn't cost too much."

Johnny Schulte's home was in St. Louis, but he had never seen Yogi play. During the regular season, even when the Yankees were in St. Louis playing the American League St. Louis Browns, he was too busy with

23

his own chores, coaching the pitchers in the Yankee bull pen. When he did get home, after the World Series, it was October, and the local baseball season was over. Still, he could talk to people, people who knew the game as it was played on the sand lots, in the public parks, among the semipro athletes; and he did.

"I like what baseball people say about you," he said to Yogi, visiting him in his home. "Of course I'd like to see you hit the ball, and do some catching, but I guess I'll rely on Leo's description. He says you're a future big league ballplayer."

Yogi listened. He knew that Schulte was there to make him some kind of offer. After his experience with the Cardinals and the Browns, he was not over-confident about the visit of the Yankee coach, but he dared to hope.

"Make it a $500 bonus," he thought to himself. "The rest doesn't matter."

And Schulte came through.

"I'm willing to sign you, without seeing you play, just on what I've heard," said the Yankee coach, "to play for Norfolk, that's in Virginia, in the Piedmont League, for $90 a month."

"What about a bonus?" pressed Yogi, holding his breath.

"Let's make it a $500 bonus."

"It's a deal!" said Yogi, perhaps a little overeagerly. "Where do I sign?"

He didn't stop to think that he was earning more than twice the money he had been offered to play for Norfolk, pulling tacks at the shoe factory. The important thing was that he had been offered that $500 bonus, exactly the bonus Joey Garagiola had been offered. The wounds to his pride were suddenly healed. The scars of those wounds would fall off quickly. He was being recognized as a professional baseball player, a player worth a $500 bonus, and that was all that mattered to young Yogi Berra.

Even Papa Pietro Berra smiled at the prospects of that $500 bonus. Maybe, he thought, baseball was not just a bum's game after all.

Yogi, the baseball contract in his pocket, went back to work at the Johansen's Shoe Company happily. In just a few short months he was to report to the Kansas City training camp at Excelsior Springs, Missouri. It was going to be difficult living through a winter of anticipation, but no matter what the weather was, snow, sleet or ice, there was always a rainbow in the sky for young Yogi. He had finally broken through. He was now a professional baseball player on his way to the big leagues. Nothing was going to stop him now, nothing.

Ironically, just before Yogi packed his things and readied himself for the spring training camp, a Western Union Telegram boy knocked at the Berra door. The telegram was for Yogi and it came from Branch Rickey. Rickey was general manager of the Brooklyn Dodgers now, and the telegram asked Yogi to report immediately to the Dodger camp in Bear Mountain, New York, where a bonus contract was waiting for him to sign.

Yogi was a bit puzzled by Branch Rickey's change of heart. It never occurred to him that with the drafting of the young men into the country's military services it was becoming more and more difficult to find youngsters for the baseball wars; that perhaps Rickey had figured that Yogi really had the potential to fill a much-needed spot in one of the Dodger's farm teams. It was enough for him that Branch Rickey was calling on him; that, for all purposes, Branch Rickey was admitting he had made an error of judgment on that dramatic day of the tryout in Sportsman's Park.

"Look at it," he said to his father, his mother, his brothers, and the smile of a deep sense of satisfaction creased his face. "Now Brooklyn wants me to play for them, too!"

Papa Pietro read the telegram.

"How much bonus?" he asked.

Papa was a practical head in the Berra family.

"He doesn't say," said Yogi. "It doesn't matter."

The only thing that mattered to Yogi was the contents of the message that had come along the Western Union wires. The Schulte contract was confirmation enough for his faith in himself as a professional baseball player. The Branch Rickey request just removed whatever lingering doubt he may have had at all about his ability to make good.

"I'm a Yankee now," he said. "I belong to the New York Yankee organization."

He would never know what kind of bonus Branch Rickey had had in mind. He would never ask about it, and nobody, neither Rickey nor anybody else in the Brooklyn Dodger organization, would tell him about it. And, as Yogi himself had said, it didn't matter.

"I belong to the New York Yankees," he said.

It was in a New York Yankee uniform that the youngster from the Hill section of St. Louis was going to make baseball history.

Chapter 4

Playing ball for Norfolk was a tremendous experience for Yogi. It was the most exciting, and at the same time, one of the most unhappy periods of his life. He was to learn a great deal from this one season with Norfolk that would stand him in good stead throughout his career in baseball.

Norfolk, Virginia, was the base for the Atlantic Fleet of the United States Navy and the Fifth Naval District Headquarters during the Second World War. Its normal population had quadrupled from some 180,000 to some three quarters of a million. Sailors were everywhere, jamming the streets. So were the hundreds of thousands of defense workers and ship construction workers, who had moved into the normally peaceful small town. The restaurants were always filled to capacity. There was always difficulty finding an empty seat in one of the few movie houses. The only entertainment readily available was the opportunity to fight some sailor or a whole batch of sailors who had been drinking too much.

"Lots of noses got punched in that town," said Yogi, "every night of the week."

It wasn't the kind of town to make a youngster of seventeen comfortable. But Yogi, away from home for the first time in his life, was interested only in making the grade with the Norfolk Tars. He had very little interest in comfort or entertainment. He just wanted to play every day with a professional baseball team.

He had no trouble making the regular line-up of the Norfolk squad. Few of the men with the Class B Piedmont League clubs had any more professional experience than Yogi had, and those that did were generally fellows who had been playing minor league ball for years and who would never climb any higher on the baseball ladder. But there were a number of other difficulties young Yogi Berra would have to deal with and control.

First there was the business of collecting the $500 bonus the Yankee coach, Johnny Schulte, had promised him. Nobody in the Norfolk front office seemed to be in a hurry to fulfill that promise, or even know about it.

Yogi was patient for a while, but he soon discovered that his salary hardly covered his living expenses. He was always short of money, and sometimes didn't have money for food.

He went directly to Jim Dawson, the general manager of the Norfolk Tars.

"Doesn't somebody around here owe me $500?" he asked; he was hungry and his hunger added to his anger.

"What are you talking about, kid?"

Dawson was a tight man with money. Five hundred dollars was a lot of money.

"Five hundred dollars? Who owes you $500?"

"I mean," said Yogi, beginning to think that he was asking the wrong man about it, "I was told I was going to get a $500 bonus."

"Yeah. Sure," said Jim Dawson. "If you last through the season."

"That isn't what Schulte promised me," snapped an angry young Berra.

"That's what I'm promising you," snapped back an equally angered Jim Dawson.

There was nothing Yogi could do about it. Eventually he did get the promised $500, but meanwhile he had to pay his rent, eat, and see an occasional movie on the $45 he was paid by the Norfolk Tars every two weeks.

He roomed with Bill Sukey, one of the Norfolk pitchers. Rent came to seven dollars a week. After the rent, there was just about a dollar a day on which to eat, see a movie, or buy a comic book. For a fellow whose mother used to feed him huge plates of antipasto, risotto, ravioli, and huge helpings of meat and potatoes and spaghetti, this starvation diet on which he was forced to live was just too much for a growing young man to take.

"I borrowed money from anybody who would lend it to me," said Berra. "I was hungry all the time, and I was broke all the time."

He even asked Mamma Berra to send him a few dollars every now and then; and she did.

"But don't let Papa know," she wrote, "or he'll make you come home."

Once, Yogi was so hungry that he went on a "hunger strike."

It was just before game time. All the players were suiting up, all the players except Yogi. He just sat himself down on a bench, clutched at his stomach and began to moan.

"What's wrong with you?" demanded Shakey Kain.

Yogi was the only catcher he had on his squad. The other two "regulars" were both out with injured hands.

"Why don't you suit up?"

"I'm sick," moaned Yogi. "Can't you see I'm sick?"

"Sick of what?"

"Sick of not eating! I'm hungry! That's what's the matter with me! I'm hungry!"

"Hungry!" shouted Shakey Kain. "Suit up! You'll eat after the game!"

"I'm not playing," groaned Yogi. "I can't play with my stomach empty. It hurts."

Kain cussed under his breath. He shoved his hand into his pocket and pulled out a dollar.

"Get yourself something to eat!" he hollered. "And get back here in a hurry!"

He didn't have to tell Yogi to hurry. Berra was up on his feet and out of the clubhouse before Kain could utter another cuss word under his breath, and headed straight for the refreshment stand.

Four hamburgers and two Cokes later Berra was back in the clubhouse and feeling much better. That night, he remembers, he was in good form. Yogi could always play better on a full stomach.

Sunday was a special day for young Berra and his stomach when he was playing for Norfolk. It was on

30

Sundays that a kind lady who had taken a special liking for the young ballplayer came to the ball park with a special gift for him, a giant size hero sandwich, Italian bread well-filled with all kinds of meat and cheese. Maybe it was only that she recognized how hungry the poor fellow was and, like a good mother, wanted to feed him.

In any case, after putting away that loaf of bread and all its goodies, Yogi was a hero on the diamond. He hit homers, triples, doubles, banged in a record-making number of runs. There were two days, when Norfolk played against the Roanoke nine, in which Yogi collected 12 hits, a double, 2 triples and 3 home runs, in addition to 6 singles. In the first of the two-day series, he batted in 13 runs. In the second game, he batted in another 10 runs.

That first year Yogi caught 111 games for the Norfolk Tars and was the spark plug of the team. He hit for a respectable average of .253, though that would be a low average for him later on in his career; and he batted home 56 runs. It was a fine record for a first season in organized baseball.

He played well enough, by mid-season, to ask the general manager Dawson for a raise, and the tight-fisted Dawson actually gave it to him. The raise amounted to five dollars a month, hardly enough to buy more than four hot dogs a week, but young Berra had taken his first step in the art and practice of contract bargaining. He would do a lot more of this kind of bargaining later on, and for numbers that made him one of baseball's highest paid players.

It was at Norfolk, too, that Yogi got to know some of the top big leaguers: Phil Rizzuto of the Yankees,

Dom DiMaggio of the Boston Red Sox, Sam Chapman of the Philadelphia Athletics, Don Padgett of the St. Louis Browns, Freddie Hutchinson of the Detroit Tigers, Vinnie Smith of the Pittsburgh Pirates, Hugh Casey of the Brooklyn Dodgers, Eddie Robinson of the Cleveland Indians, and others. They were all in the United States Navy at the time, playing ball for the Service before they went into active combat duty, and Yogi got to meet them all when the Norfolk Tars played the Norfolk Naval Station Training team in an exhibition game.

Yogi talked to them all. He was always a great talker, as every player, manager, coach, and umpire in the big leagues would soon discover. He also talked to Warrant Officer Gary Brodie, who coached the Naval team, and Brodie urged young Berra to select the Navy for his service when he was called up in the draft.

"I'll be losing most of these boys," said Brodie. "They're all going to be shipped out soon, and I can use your bat, when you join up."

As a matter of fact Yogi's draft number had already come up. He had requested his St. Louis draft board to send on the necessary papers to Norfolk, his current residence, and the postponement gave him just about enough time to finish his season with the Tars, enough time to collect that elusive $500 bonus. Brodie's talk sounded good to Berra. He was as eager as any young fellow to serve his country in the war, and the idea of serving it by playing ball, even if for only a little while, seemed like a perfect set-up.

Warrant Officer Gary Brodie did put in a bid for Yogi with the recruiting authorities. And, at Richmond, Virginia, where Yogi took and passed his physical examination, young Berra asked that he be put into the Navy.

"Navy," wrote the recruiting officer on the official papers; but then Yogi had second thoughts.

"How much time do I have before I have to report?" he asked.

"A week," snapped the officer. "That's what the Navy gives you. A week."

"How much does the Army give you?" asked Yogi. His mind was operating fast.

"A month," said the officer.

Yogi had been away from home for a long time. He had gotten over the initial homesickness of the young fellow away from his family for the first time, but he thought he would enjoy seeing his father, his mother, his brothers, and sister again, and for a little more than a week.

"I've changed my mind," he said to the man behind the desk. "I'll take the Army."

The officer looked up at Berra, quizzically. "What kind of nut is this I'm dealing with," he as much as thought to himself.

He was kinder, if a bit cold and short, in what he actually said.

"I'm sorry, fellow."

He indicated the papers on his desk.

"You're in the Navy now."

One week later, to the day, Yogi Berra began his six weeks of boot training at the Bainbridge Naval Base in Maryland. Every day, during those six weeks, except for the seven days he was away on an emergency furlough, he eagerly looked through what little mail he got for the call Warrant Officer Gary Brodie had promised and the quick transfer to Norfolk and the Naval Base ball team. But the letter he expected from Brodie didn't come. It never came.

The emergency furlough Berra received, with the aid of the American Red Cross, came about when Yogi learned that his mother was to undergo a breast operation. For seven days he was back in St. Louis, shuttling between the hospital, where his mother lay, and his home on Elizabeth Street. It wasn't until his mother left the hospital and the doctors promised her recovery, that he returned to Bainbridge. Yogi was constantly worried about his mother's health and condition. He was deeply attached to her, as he was to the rest of his family. Family loyalty, among his other loyalties, was always a strong point in Yogi's character. It was his loyalty—to family, to friends, to his ball team, to the game—that made Yogi Berra one of the most respected, most liked, even most loved of men, on or off the diamond.

Back at the Bainbridge Naval Base, Yogi completed his boot training, after which he was shipped to Little Creek, Virginia, for amphibious training.

It was at Little Creek that Yogi's greatest and most dangerous experience, during his stint with the Navy, was to begin.

Chapter 5

For the first month at Little Creek, Yogi did little more than loaf around the barracks, read comic books, eat at the mess hall, and go to the movies they were always showing at the post. Little Creek was practically next door to Norfolk, but Norfolk, with its jammed streets, crowded restaurants, and drunks was no novelty to Yogi. Of course, he was better off in his Navy uniform than he had been as a civilian when he played for the Tars; he could eat all he wanted to eat at the Navy base and the movies were provided free of charge; but he was bored. Yogi was young, healthy, and he both liked and needed action. There was no action for Yogi at Little Creek. He was bored.

Suddenly, however, the situation took an about face. Action, and dangerous action, was to become the routine for Yogi, and not exactly as he might have expected it.

He was sitting in the post movie house watching a cowboy and Indian flick or, as Yogi thinks he recalls, Clark Gable and Spencer Tracy in *Boom Town*. Which-

35

ever it was, the reel abruptly stopped and a "Hear this! Hear this!" came over the loud speakers. "All enlisted men return to their barracks! All enlisted men return to their barracks!"

Calls like that came often enough at Little Creek, and generally they didn't mean very much more than a roll call. This time it was different.

"We want volunteers. We want volunteers for a new kind of Navy boat, the Landing Craft Support Small Rocket Launcher, the LCSS Rocket Launcher. We're calling for volunteers. If you want to volunteer, report to your commanding officer. Repeat. If you want to volunteer for the LCSS Rocket Launcher, report immediately to your commanding officer."

Perhaps it was the promise of escape from boredom that got Yogi moving. Maybe it was the sound of glamour the word "rocket" implied. In any case, Berra reported to his commanding officer and volunteered to serve with the new Naval craft. It was the end of doing nothing in the Navy for the young fellow.

"You're going to see action," announced the officer in charge of the first meeting of the volunteers, rather ominously. "You're not just going to be standing by, watching the action."

That became clear to the volunteers with their first look at the LCSS. The boat was just 36 feet long. One officer and five enlisted men constituted its crew. Each side of the Rocket Launcher was armed with six machine guns and twelve rockets. It was an invasion boat. It was destined for the mightiest and most important invasions of World War II, D-Day and Omaha Beach. It was the smallest boat in that invasion, nothing more than "a platform to carry a whole lot of live fire-

36

crackers," as Yogi was to put it, but its role in that invasion was to be heroic.

For five weeks, Seaman 2nd Class Lawrence Peter Berra and his comrades trained intensively and secretly at Little Creek. The whole operation was top-drawer secret. The volunteers were strictly forbidden to mention anything about their activities, anything about their training, anything about their boats, in any letters to home, or anywhere else. The LCSS was to be a surprise weapon against the Nazi enemy, guarding the English Channel coast of Nazi-held France.

After five weeks of secret training as a machine gunner on the secret vessel, Yogi, along with his comrades and Rocket Launcher, were moved to Lido Beach on Long Island, from where they were to embark on a destination already determined by the Allied Invasion Team. But embarkation was still three weeks off, and for those three weeks the volunteers were kept busy with one kind of detail or another. Yogi says he put on five pounds at Lido Beach, working as a soda jerk in a ship store. Yogi would never give up his appetite for hot dogs, sodas, ice creams, and the like.

Bayonne, New Jersey, was the next stop on the itinerary of the volunteers, and here they were put on board an LST headed for Boston, where they joined a convoy and moved on through the Atlantic to Glasgow, Scotland. Like a good many of the other young men, Yogi was terribly seasick on the ride from Bayonne to Boston, but he found his sea legs soon enough and, except for lack of sleep during the voyage, the passage across the ocean was without any incident.

From Glasgow, it was a train ride to Plymouth, the age-old port on the Devonshire coast of England. Here,

Yogi waited with his comrades for D-Day and for perhaps the most exciting and certainly most dangerous adventure of his life.

D-Day was set for June 4, 1944, by General Dwight D. Eisenhower, the Allied Commander-in-Chief. Everyone involved knew how perilous the operation was to be. Thousands of men would lose their lives in the invasion of Omaha Beach, many thousands more would be wounded, seriously wounded, maimed for the rest of their years. There was a lot of praying in the English port town the day and the night of June 3. A man had to make things right with his Maker before he went into battle. Perhaps the good Lord would turn that bullet aside, send the shrapnel on some other path, let the bombs explode in some other place.

Yogi knew well enough that he wasn't going on a picnic, that there was going to be a lot of shooting and a lot of killing, that some of the friends he had made in training were going to die. But Yogi was young, and the young are not inclined to dwell on death, certainly not on their own death. The thought that he might die in battle never really occurred to him for more than a fleeting moment. He was a good Catholic. His faith in the Almighty was enough to quiet any fears that might have arisen in him, but there wasn't a hint of fear in Yogi's body. He said his prayers, all right; but Yogi always said his prayers. The Good Lord, he knew, would take care of him. It was a good feeling to have, the moments before the invasion. During the invasion there would be little time to think of anything but the big job on hand.

But June 4 came and went, and there was no invasion. Near-hurricane winds and torrential rains made it impossible. Bucking the winds and the rains would have made only for a disastrous effort and a dreadful failure. D-Day was reset for June 6. Waiting made things no easier for the men. If anything, it increased the already near-breaking point tensions.

Early in the morning of June 5, General Eisenhower made the June 6 invasion date firm. Reports indicated that the weather would be good that morning, and for at least the next thirty-six hours. Bad weather or good, however, the Allied Armies, Navies, and Air Forces would strike on the morning of June 6. Those were the orders from the high command.

On the night of June 5, the LCSS Rocket Ship, with Yogi Berra at his machine gun, was loaded onto the U.S.S. *Bayfield*. No one on board that ship that night slept. Everyone checked his gear to see that it was in perfect working condition. Last minute instructions were repeated and repeated. Every man was alert, on his toes, and ready to go.

In the darkness of the early morning hours of June 6, on schedule, the massive Allied fleet took off for France.

General Eisenhower had addressed all his men on all the ships only hours earlier.

"This is one of the greatest moments in the history of man. Every man of us must do his part. Every man will be responsible for our victory."

It was an inspiring, brief talk. Ike had a way with his men. He buoyed up their spirits, gave them a cause, and because they knew that he was always with them, they fought the better for it.

At four-thirty that morning six tiny LCSS boats

were lowered out of the *Bayfield* and into the English Channel. Allied planes had been pounding the proposed landing spots for hours now, and they continued to pound them with all the bombs they could carry. The task of the LCSS boats was to hit the German machine-gun emplacements with their rockets, clearing the area of enemy fire so that the landing G.I.'s could make the beach and dig in—with a better chance of survival. The LCSS boats, headed straight for what was to be called, from that day on, Omaha Beach.

The six LCSS Rocket boats worked according to plan. One hundred yards apart, they rushed through the waters, and held their fire until they were only 300 yards from the shore. They zigged, they zagged, anything to make it more difficult for enemy shells to find them, and the German big guns began to look for them almost before they could be deposited into the Channel by the *Bayfield*. They got to within the 300 yards of the beach, let go with all their rockets aimed at the Nazi emplacements, retreated to reload, came back to within 300 yards of the sand again, and once more hammered the German position with their deadly rockets.

For something like six hours the little expendable LCSS ships, with their expendable crews of six, moved in and out, toward the beach, away from it, and back again.

Perhaps Yogi, who was just eighteen years old, was just too young or just didn't know enough to be scared. Maybe he didn't have time to be scared.

There was one moment when all the fire and flame of the invasion and the efforts of the Germans to stop it, got to the young sailor. He had to have a look-see at all the fireworks and he poked his head up over the side of the LCSS.

"Get your head down!" barked the lieutenant of his squad, "if you want to keep it!"

Yogi wanted to keep his head. He ducked his head down and had to be satisfied with a sky view of that great Normandy, D-Day invasion.

It was a bloody battle and the Allies paid heavily for it. But it was a necessary battle if the tide were to be turned against Hitler and his Nazi marauders. It was a battle that needed to be won, and the Allies did win it. Omaha Beach was secured, and the Allies were landed on the coast of France. The tide of the battle for Europe had turned.

For the next eleven days, the LCSS crews worked the Channel. They constituted a messenger service between the Omaha and the Utah beachheads of the Allied Forces. They guided the new ships, with their cargoes of G.I.'s and munitions, through the mine fields dotting the Channel. They were constantly on the alert for German air raids, ducking, weaving, firing their anti-aircraft at them.

There was precious little sleep for the crews of the LCSS boats during that stint. There was little time to wash up and nobody cared about shaving. All they had to eat were K-rations, and little time in which to eat them.

When they were finally released from their duties, after almost two full weeks, Yogi, and everyone else in the crew, just flopped into their bunks and passed out. Every now and then, the beep-beep of an alarm would sound off, warning them of enemy planes overhead, but no one seemed to care any more.

"If it hits," said Yogi, "let it hit. I can't move."

As he said, later on, talking of those eventful days, "I was just too tired to be scared."

He was promoted to Seaman 1st Class, and was soon on his way, with the rest of his crew, to Bizerte, Africa, for his next stint—the invasion of southern France. In this invasion, Yogi almost got himself killed.

This time, the beachhead chosen was close to the big French seaport of Marseilles. The code name for this invasion was "Yellow Beach." The target chosen especially for assault by Yogi's LCSS was a huge resort hotel where the Germans were entrenched and well-equipped with machine guns and mortars.

The LCSS peppered that hotel with rockets. Behind the LCSS was a squadron of British rocket boats, reinforcing the American fire power. Behind the British, the infantry men came on their jammed-to-the-hilt landing craft.

The firing from all sides was tremendous. All of a sudden someone on the LCSS bobbing around in the Mediterranean yelled, "Heads down!"

Everyone on the boat hit the deck. Yogi let go of the rocket he was loading and dived under a gun mount.

It was a British shell, fired by a British rocket ship, misaimed and heading straight for the American LCSS.

"I felt that this was going to be the end," said Yogi, later, talking of his war years, "and there wasn't hardly time enough for a Hail Mary!"

However, nobody's name was on that British shell. It landed in the water no more than a yard off the stern of the American rocket launcher—close enough to finish off its whole crew if it hadn't been a dud. The gigantic splash it made in the water was enough to set the small LCSS bouncing and rocking, but it didn't explode and none of the American crew suffered more than a bad scare.

Still, it was as close to death as Yogi came in the European Theater of War, though he did get nicked by a German machine-gun bullet, before the LCSS rockets cleaned out the Nazi nest of guns and gunners. Actually, he could have collected a Purple Heart for it, but he never applied for the medal.

"I didn't want to worry my Mamma," he said.

But that was the total extent of the damage the Nazis could inflict on the young fellow from the Hill section of St. Louis. There wasn't another scratch on him for all of his perilous exploits in the Channel and in the Mediterranean, in the two great Allied victories at Omaha Beach and again at Yellow Beach, in the southern belly of France.

There were easier moments for Yogi in his European stretch of service. There was the moving reception he received, along with his comrades-in-arms, from the liberated French, when Yellow Beach was emptied of its Nazi occupation force and the Americans paraded through the town victoriously.

"One minute it was all shooting and killing," said Yogi. "The next thing you know, there are all the Frenchmen and women and kids, too, coming out of all those shelled hotels with bottles of wine and bouquets of flowers for you, with kisses, and with tears in their eyes."

The sudden contrast between war and peace was an

overwhelming experience for the young fellow. He was learning of depths of emotion he had never known before, emotions not easy for an eighteen-year-old to fully understand.

There was his trip through Italy, too, when he was stationed in Naples. It was at Naples that he bumped into an old buddy of his, Bob Cocaterra from the Hill section of St. Louis, now with the U. S. Army.

"Hey!"

"Hey, Yogi!"

"What are you doing here?"

"I'm driving this jeep to Milan."

"How about taking me to Rome?"

Yogi, the good Catholic, had heard about Rome as long as he could remember, Rome and the Vatican, where the Pope lived.

"It's all right with me," said Bob Cocaterra, "if it's all right with your C.O."

Yogi got to his C.O., fast.

The C.O. was noncommittal.

"I don't know when they're shipping us out again. They don't tell me. Maybe it'll be tomorrow. Maybe we'll be hanging around down here for another month. Do what you like."

Yogi did what he liked. He had already been awarded a Distinguished Unit Citation, two battle stars, an ETO ribbon, and a Good Conduct Medal. He figured they wouldn't do too much to him, if he took a short absence without leave. He headed for Rome with his pal.

When they got to Rome, Bob suggested that Yogi go on with him to Milan, maybe look into the town of Malvaglio, the town his mother and father came from.

"They're still fighting up that way," said Yogi.

He shook his head, thanked his old buddy for the lift, then spent about a week in the capital city of Italy, taking in all the sights. One day during his stay in Rome he got a look at the Pope, standing on the balcony at the Vatican, and this was an especially pleasing moment for Yogi. It was something he could tell his mother, something that would please her no end.

Yogi got back to Naples feeling very good about his adventure. He felt even better when he discovered there had been no change in the situation for his detachment. There was, as a matter of fact, little left for his crew, with its special rocket assignment, to do. The LCSS Rocket Launchers had done their work, and done it well. Its crews were to be transferred to other areas and other war-time labors.

Toward the end of that year, the LCSS men were shipped to Oran, Africa, without any special assignment. In Oran, Yogi went to a midnight mass on Christmas Eve. On New Year's Eve, the entire detachment was ordered to board ship and sail back to the United States. For all purposes, Yogi's active service in the Allied war effort had come to an end.

Chapter 6

Back in the States, and with a month's leave, Yogi fattened up on his mother's good cooking. But he had been told that he had to report to New London, Connecticut, at the end of his leave, and that worried him a bit. New London was a submarine base. The idea of fighting a war under water didn't appeal to him. Yogi always liked to see where he was going.

His worrying, however, wasn't at all necessary or called for. Somewhere in the long list of questionnaires he had filled in for the Navy, he had indicated a preference to serve in sports and recreation. Personal preferences generally didn't count much with the officers and men in charge of Navy personnel, but, by sheer accident or extremely good luck, that was where Yogi found himself in New London: assigned to Sports and Recreation.

He hoped to play with the baseball team on the base. It was a pretty good ball club, with Lieutenant James Gleeson, formerly of the Cincinnati Reds and the Chicago Cubs, its manager. But, in true-to-form Navy fashion, Yogi was assigned to be a maintenance man at the base's movie house. His job was to sweep out the house every night and to fix anything, like chairs, that had been broken. It wasn't bad, seeing all the movies he wanted to see, but he wanted to play baseball. He kept bothering the personnel officer, Commander Robert H. Barnes.

"I'm a professional baseball player. I belong to the New York Yankees. Why don't you send me over to Jimmy Gleeson. He can use me."

Commander Barnes looked over the squat, chunky, "fire hydrant," and couldn't see him as a ballplayer. But Yogi was persistent, and Barnes finally acquiesced to the sailor's request.

Gleeson looked at Yogi and his reaction was the same as Barnes's.

"You're a ballplayer?" he said, the doubt clear as a bell in his throat.

"I belong to the Yankees," said Yogi. "I played a year with the Norfolk Tars before the Navy caught up with me."

"Yeah?" said Gleeson, looking through the papers Yogi had brought with him from the personnel office. "It says here that you're a boxer."

"I did some boxing, but I'm Yankee property, like I told you. I'm a professional ballplayer."

Gleeson still studied the papers on his desk. It was easier than looking at this heavy-set kid who said he belonged to the Yankees.

"I can hit," said Yogi. "I'm a pretty good hitter."

"Yeah?" said Gleeson.

"I hit .253 for Norfolk," said Yogi, "but I batted in 56 runs."

47

"Sure," said Gleeson. He was certain that the young sailor was exaggerating, but he wouldn't say so.

He called in his assistant, Ray Volpe, who had pitched for the Kansas City Blues, and together they quizzed young Berra for most of half an hour. The questions were all on baseball, facts and figures, averages and league scores, and nobody knew baseball facts and history better than Yogi Berra.

Ultimately, Gleeson and Volpe were satisfied that Yogi was telling most of the truth about himself, if not all of it, and he was to report to April baseball practice at the base.

Seaman 1st Class Berra was delighted. Baseball was even more joyful to Yogi than perhaps eating. He was going to be a ballplayer again. He was going to be swinging that bat again. Gleeson had two seasoned catchers for his squad, Joe Glenn of the Yankees and Tony Anselmo of the Pacific Coast League Sacramento club. Manager Gleeson watched Yogi wallop the ball in the very first practice session, and for all Berra's lack of finesse, he knew that he had a fine hitter for his team. He put Yogi out in the outfield, and he worried every time a ball was hit out his way. Yogi had his problems with a fly ball, but his big bat would help the team.

Later in the season, Glenn was shipped out, Anselmo broke an ankle, and Yogi got to be the team's regular catcher. He was still erratic when throwing the ball to second base, to nail a man trying to steal, but he could handle the pitchers, and they all liked him. There wasn't a game the Raiders played (the Raiders was the nickname for Gleeson's squad) in which Yogi wasn't in the line-up; and every game they played was against good semipro and other service teams.

There were other baseball games Yogi played at this time when he was off duty. There was always a semipro team eager to use his bat, and Yogi would pick up an extra fifty dollars on his leave days away from the base.

"I was glad to send a little extra money home," he said. That was what he did with the money he made playing semipro ball on his days off. "Mom's illness had cost the family a lot of money, and they could use whatever I sent them."

Perhaps the most important game, however, on Yogi's schedule that year was the exhibition game the Raiders played against the New York Giants.

Mel Ott was the manager of the Giants at the time and he was immediately attracted to Yogi as he watched him hammer the ball over the fence in batting practice. He watched, with added interest, as Yogi banged out three hits against the Giant pitcher Ace Adams—three out of four times at bat.

"He belongs to the Yankees," said Gleeson, observing Mel Ott's reaction to the youngster's bat.

"That was a wild pitch he hit," said Ott, as if he hadn't heard Gleeson.

"He'll hit anything that comes near the plate, and a lot that's off the plate," said the manager of the Raiders. "But he hits it. He's awkward, can't throw, but he has the quickest wrist action I've ever seen. He's going to be a great hitter in the big leagues."

Mel Ott knew a fine baseball prospect when he saw one. The day he got back to New York from New London and the exhibition game with the Raiders, he went in to see Larry MacPhail, who was president and manager of the New York Yankees at the time.

"You've got a kid catching in the Navy up in New London," he said. "He belongs to you. I'm ready to give you $50,000 for him."

Larry MacPhail, who was a shrewd dealer, didn't know anything about a young catcher in New London, but he wasn't going to let Mel Ott know that.

"That kid catcher?" he queried, stalling for time.

"Berra. They call him Yogi Berra."

"Yeah," said MacPhail. "I know who you mean."

Of course he didn't.

"Fifty thousand dollars?"

"That's what I said."

"Maybe you've got yourself a deal," said MacPhail. "Let me think about it?"

He thought about it fast enough. As soon as Mel Ott was outside the door, he called for Paul Krichell, the Yankee scout.

"Who's this kid catcher in the Navy in New London?" he demanded. "Mel Ott wants him. What do you know about him? Is he that good? Ott wants to shell out $50,000. Maybe we've got ourselves a star and we don't know it?"

Krichell knew every player on every farm club the Yankees owned. He gave MacPhail a quick run-down on young Berra, what he could do, and his potential.

"Get him down here," said MacPhail. "Let me take a look at him."

Krichell sent a wire off to Yogi posthaste, and Yogi was thrilled to read the invitation to meet with the general manager and president of the big league New York Yankees. He didn't have any idea of why he had been asked to come to New York, or why MacPhail wanted to see him; it was enough for him that the big boss of the Yankees even knew about him. The first chance he had to make the trip to the big city, he took it.

"I'm Yogi Berra. You asked me to come to see you."

MacPhail did a double take. This kid didn't even look like a professional ballplayer. In fact, in his tight white sailor pants, sailor hat, and with his odd walk, he looked like a small-time burlesque comic.

The Yankee manager was sure Mel Ott had made a mistake, and that he had made a worse mistake in not taking the $50,000 the Giants' manager had offered him for this clumsy-looking Navy man.

"O.K.," he said, fighting to collect his cool. "Sit down and tell me something about yourself."

Yogi was a great conversationalist, but he wasn't used to talking about himself. Still, his enthusiasm for the game must have impressed MacPhail.

"When do you get out of service?" he asked.

"I'm not sure," said Yogi.

"O.K. When you're discharged from the Navy we'll see what you can do in Newark."

Newark was a top Yankee farm club in the International League. Yogi was elated. But he wasn't so elated that he lost the business sense he had picked up battling for something to eat, fighting for that salary boost with the Norfolk Tars.

"Who's paying my expenses for this trip?" he asked MacPhail.

Yogi said that he figured the Yankees had more money than he did. And Larry MacPhail, the broad grin on his face, said, "Maybe I didn't think much of him when he walked into my office, but when he asked me to pay for his train ticket, I didn't have to be told that I was dealing with a professional ballplayer."

May 6, 1946, just six days before his twenty-first birthday, Yogi Berra was released from the Navy. He celebrated his birthday with his mother and father and brothers and sister in St. Louis. Then, since he had received no official word from the Yankee front office, he readied himself for Kansas City, where he expected he was still on that club's roster.

But before he could run through all his farewells to his family and friends on the Hill, MacPhail came through with his promise. A telegram, delivered to the Berra home, ordered Yogi to report to Newark.

Yogi didn't know it at the time, but he was less than a full step from the New York Yankees and the realization of a great career.

Chapter 7

Yogi Berra reported to the Newark Bears on the eve of an important three-game series against Rochester. There were no bands waiting to greet him. George Selkirk, who had played in the outfield for the New York Yankees and who was now managing the Bears, took one look at Yogi and, like everyone else on his squad, wondered what kind of fool trick MacPhail was playing on him. Yogi still looked like anything but a professional ballplayer. He never would.

"Give him a suit," said Selkirk to Jimmy Mack, the Newark Bears' club boy, much as to say, "Get rid of this kid who looks like somebody who has lost his way out of a wrestling ring."

Anyway, that was the way the clubhouse manager Jimmy Mack took it. He gave Yogi an old uniform that didn't even have a number on its back. He gave him a cap that was too small.

"Give me a cap I can wear," said Yogi.

The clubhouse boy, without so much as a glance at the ballplayer, split the seam down the back of the cap and handed it back to him.

And that was about all Yogi was going to take.

He made a heap of the uniform and cap and tossed them both at the boy.

"Give me a new uniform," he said, quietly but firmly. "I'm not here to try out for this club. I play for it."

He was given a uniform that fit; but it was a while before he actually broke into the Bears' line-up.

Newark had a very good club that year. They had Buddy Hassett, Bobby Brown, Joe Collins, Allie Clark, Jack Phillips, Frank Coleman, and Vic Raschi, all big league material. They also had two pretty good catchers in Mike Garbark and Charlie Fallon. George Selkirk wasn't eager to put Yogi into his line-up. MacPhail, however, had other ideas.

Bill Dickey, one of the greatest catchers in the history of the game, and always a big bat for the New York Yankees, was near the end of a brilliant career. He was just about ready to hang up his glove and his spikes, and MacPhail knew that the Yankees desperately needed a catcher. It made him all the more eager to see what this young Berra could do, whether he was worth the $50,000 Mel Ott had offered him for the farmhand. He called up Selkirk and gave him the orders.

"Put that kid Yogi Berra into the line-up."

It was in the first game of a double-header that Selkirk followed MacPhail's orders, using Yogi as a pinch hitter; and Yogi, in his first time up for the Bears, smashed out a hit.

Yogi's style at the plate was unorthodox, clumsy, but Selkirk saw something in his baseball reactions, as he saw him round first base, head for second, then

54

pull back in time. The kid certainly didn't look like a ballplayer but he seemed to have the right instincts; and he could hit.

Selkirk put him in the line-up for the second game of the double-header, and Yogi smashed out 2 hits out of his official 3 times at bat and a base on balls on his fourth trip to the plate. He was still reaching for the high ones, the low ones, the wide ones, all pitches out of the strike zone, but he was slugging the ball and getting on base. From that day on, Yogi Berra was the regular catcher for George Selkirk's Newark Bears, and Larry MacPhail was pleased with all the reports he got from the club. He certainly hadn't made a mistake turning down Mel Ott's $50,000 offer for the sailor boy.

There were others in the International League who were considerably impressed by Yogi's bat that season. Bucky Harris, who was the general manager of the Buffalo club that year, said he would have liked to have shot Berra every time he came up against one of his pitchers. Clay Hopper, who managed Montreal, devised a shift in an effort to stop Yogi. He moved his right fielder over to protect the right-field foul line. His first baseman hugged the line, too. The second baseman shifted right, and the shortstop played the second-base position, every time Yogi got up to the plate. It was the kind of shift that Lou Boudreau, managing the Cleveland Indians, used some time later to try to stop the .400 bat of the Hall-of-Famer Ted Williams.

It didn't help Lou Boudreau much. It didn't help Clay Hopper. Yogi slammed out 5 hits in 7 times at bat the first time Hopper shifted his players in a double-header.

Yankee scouts had said that Yogi could hit anything, and when that chunky 195 pound guy, with the big hands and quick wrists got to hit, he did. What they didn't know at the time was that they had sold the Yankees on one of the most instinctive, intuitive baseball minds in the history of the game. One quick look at him and you thought you were looking at a fellow who didn't even know what it was to think. But Yogi's mind was always sizing up a play, working, thinking, analyzing. And as he gained in experience and ability, the better and the quicker he became at summing up a baseball situation and making the right play at the right time.

He may have been slow of speech and his vocabulary was limited—after all he had had little enough schooling—but he got along famously with the smartest player on the Newark Bears' squad, Bobby Brown, who was studying to become a doctor of medicine. They roomed together and, if their reading interests were different, they were great pals. One of the results of their friendship was the first and maybe the most famous of the kind of stories the newspapers were going to print about Yogi for a long time.

It seems that both Berra and Brown were in their hotel room, reading. Yogi, as usual, was reading one of his favorite comic books. Bobby Brown was deep in some thick medical book. Bobby got a little tired, it was late, closed his book and said, "Let's turn the lights out."

"Just a minute," begged Yogi. "I'm almost finished."

Another minute or two, and Yogi closed up his comic book.

"This was a good story," he said, with much satisfaction. "How did your book come out?"

There are countless stories about Yogi along this line, and a good many of them are true. Yogi was an innocent in many ways—but never on the diamond. It is true that when trying to throw out a man running for second base he hit an umpire—and that umpire was a good ten feet from the base—but he also has the record for executing double plays; grabbing a bunt fast and putting the tag on the batter, then turning around to tag the base-runner sliding into home plate.

Yogi was in 77 games that season with Newark. He hit for an average of .314, despite a bad slump in the last weeks of the schedule. He hammered out 15 home runs and his bat drove in 59 runs. His hitting undoubtedly was largely responsible for Newark's getting into the International League play-offs, but more than Yogi's bat was needed to head off the Montreal club with Jackie Robinson, Johnny Jorgensen, Al Campanis, Lew Riggs, Tom Tatum, Marv Rackley, Les Burge, and George Shuba on their squad.

Montreal took four games out of six, and that eliminated the Newark Bears from the play-offs, and ended their season. Yogi didn't like to lose, and he felt pretty bad about the loss to the Canadian team. It didn't help to know that the umpire made a miscall to give Montreal the last game, a call that directly involved Yogi.

Tatum, the Montreal star, was rounding the bases, trying to score on a double off the scoreboard. The ball—which Frank Coleman threw from the outfield

57

like a strike—Tatum, and Yogi's glove came together and apparently all at the same instant.

Artie Gore, who was umpiring in the minor league at the time, signaled, "Safe!" and Yogi all but jumped out of his shoes.

"What do you mean safe? He's out by a mile!"

He rushed at the umpire, using all the words he had learned on the streets of the Hill and in the Navy, ready to "kill the umpire."

"Some guys grabbed me," said Yogi. "Else I would have hit him for sure."

Nor was Yogi the only Newark ballplayer ready to commit mayhem on the umpire. They were all out there, hollering and screaming. Montreal had to call the police to escort Artie Gore off the playing field, but the umpire stuck to his guns.

"Berra juggled the ball. It was in the air, when Tatum hit the plate."

And that Tatum run was the one that won the game and the series for Montreal. It was also largely responsible for the biggest baseball fine Yogi had ever received: $500.

"I was lucky," said Yogi, still boiling. "If I hit him, I might have been thrown out of baseball."

He was luckier than he thought at the time. The Yankee front office, undoubtedly pleased with the spunk, the courage, the fight of its young Newark catcher, paid that fine for Yogi.

There was even more good news for young Berra at the end of that 1946 season. The Yankees, well out of the pennant race by this time, called up Yogi Berra, Frank Coleman, Bobby Brown, and Vic Raschi for immediate duty.

With something less than two years of minor league ball, the kid who wasn't supposed to do better than Triple-A, according to that wise old man of baseball, Branch Rickey, was a major leaguer. If Yogi was overwhelmed by this rapid progress into the big time, he didn't show it. He was too wise in the ways of the game to go on a wild celebration because of his elevation to the club that Babe Ruth, Lou Gehrig, Joe DiMaggio, and other greats had made. He knew that being called up to the Yankees didn't guarantee that he would remain with the team. He knew, most of all, that he would have to prove that the Yankees hadn't made a mistake, that they needed him. It wasn't a lack of confidence that occupied the young Berra. He had plenty of confidence in himself, in his glove, and especially in his bat. It was just ordinary common sense, with which Yogi was much endowed. He knew where he was going. It was most important to him to know the road, how to get there.

Frank Coleman, Bobby Brown, and Yogi stood in the grandstand at Yankee Stadium, Sunday morning, on the eve of a double-header. It was their first visit to the stadium as Yankees. Maybe Coleman and Brown were swallowed in dreams of glory in a Yankee uniform. Yogi had noted that the right-field fence was 296 feet from home plate, that it was going to take a good clout to hit the ball out of the ball park. It was the physical, the practical matters involved in the game that interested the young fellow; that and food.

His observations made and duly analyzed, the practical matters of the diamond attended to, Yogi turned to the needs of his stomach.

"When do we eat?" he asked. "Do you think they'll sell us some hot dogs at the refreshment concession?"

It was typical of Berra not to make a fuss about things, when no fuss was called for. It was typical of Berra to look for food, find it, and eat it, when he was hungry.

It was also typical of Yogi that no situation, new or old, no matter how critical or even dangerous, would set his stomach quivering, his hands shaking. He was one of those people who remain calm and serene in any situation.

It was this nerve, this patience that would stand him in good stead throughout his great career in baseball, win a ball game, win a series, and, on more than one occasion in his long years in the game, win a championship and the pennant.

Chapter 8

There weren't too many fans at Yankee Stadium the first time Yogi Berra came to bat in a Yankee uniform. The New York club was well out of the race for the American League pennant and attendance had dwindled considerably in the last days of the season. But those who did sit in the stands and in the bleachers of the home that Babe Ruth made saw baseball history in the making.

Real Yankee fans, like all other fans of the game, knew every player on the club, his batting average, his home-run record, how many bases he had stolen. They also knew the records and prowess of the better players around the league. There wasn't too much, if anything, however, they knew about the farm club teams and their players, except for what they read in the sports columns. Yogi Berra was almost completely unknown when he ambled toward the plate, swinging two bats in his left hand. From their distance from the field, the fans couldn't very well see his face, but he looked a little too heavy, too squat, to be a Yankee. Yankees were known for the grace with which they slammed the ball, played the field, made those impossible plays, ran the bases.

"Berra? Where did he come from?"

"Newark?"

"Hope he can hit the ball. Looks kind of small for a Yankee batter."

He may have looked small walking up to the plate, dropping one of the two bats he carried on the way, but if Jesse Flores, pitching for Connie Mack's Philadelphia Athletics that afternoon, had any kind of judgment he couldn't miss the determination in the young fellow's face.

How do you pitch to a rookie? No one really has the book on him.

Flores tried him with a fast one, cutting a corner of the plate.

Yogi watched it go by for a strike.

Buddy Rosar, an ex-Yankee, was catching for the Athletics.

"This ain't Newark," he said, tossing the ball back to his pitcher.

Yogi stepped out of the batter's box. He took a couple of practice swings, loosened up, stepped back in the box.

"They tell me you've got a ball team in Philadelphia," he quipped.

"You'll learn a lot up here," said Rosar, "if they ever let you stay up here."

"I'm staying here, all right," came back Yogi, and he showed everybody in the park that afternoon he meant it—on the next pitch.

Rosar signaled for a curve. You've got to be able

to hit a curve ball if you mean to stay in the big time.

Flores wound up and came in with his big curve ball, low and a bit inside. Berra followed the ball well, snapped his wrist, met that inside curve, and drove the ball, high over the right field wall and into the stands. Home run!

Yogi was one of the greatest natural hitters in the history of baseball. He was the kind of hitter others stop to watch when he takes pregame batting practice, as they used to watch Babe Ruth belt them out in the batting cage, or Ted Williams, Joe DiMaggio, and very few other great natural batters. It is the sharp eye, powerful shoulders, and strong wrists, combined with a fearlessness and determination, of course, that make the great batsmen, and Yogi was endowed with all these natural elements. When he crashed his big bat into a high fast ball, the ball never had a chance. Yogi's quick wrists and powerful shoulders drove the ball right out of the park.

Yogi controlled his smile, a little bit, as he trotted around the bases, but the din of approval from the stands was beautiful music to his ears. He felt sure that that four-base clout was going to keep him close to the Yankee roster, if not in it.

MacPhail, it was reported, watching the young fellow come into home plate, after cracking out a homer on his very first time at bat in the major leagues, turned in his box and said to anybody who cared to listen, "And Mel Ott wanted me to sell him for $50,000!"

Yogi played in seven games for the New York Yankees at the end of that 1946 season. He came to bat

22 times, got 8 hits, one of them a double, 2 of them home runs, for a batting average of .364. There was no question, at least in MacPhail's mind, that Yogi Berra was going to rejoin the Yankees in spring training, come 1947.

Larry MacPhail had a flare for the dramatic. He organized an early prespring training tour for the Yankee club which was to begin in San Juan, Puerto Rico, to include three exhibition games with the Brooklyn Dodgers in Caracas, Venezuela, and wind up in Havana, Cuba. The veterans on the club didn't care for MacPhail's tour, but Yogi loved it. It meant that much more baseball and, at that moment, not yet twenty-two years old, nothing was more important than baseball.

The Yankees had three managers during the long 1946 season. They had started with Joe McCarthy, played under Bill Dickey for a while, and finished with Johnny Neun.

In 1947 Bucky Harris was managing the New York club, and he had seen Yogi play when he was general manager for the International League Buffalo club. He knew Yogi had numerous shortcomings, but he respected Yogi's big bat and fully intended to take advantage of it.

"I've got two fine catchers in Aaron Robinson and Sherm Lollar," said Harris, "I'll put you out in right field."

"I don't care where I play," Yogi said, "just so long as I play."

The Yankees had an outstanding team. Joe DiMaggio, Tommy Henrich, Charlie ("King Kong") Keller, Phil Rizzuto, Joe Gordon, Spud Chandler, Red

Ruffing, and the addition of Vic Raschi to its pitching staff, made the New York club a potential pennant winner. The Yankee squad, as always, had its full quota of some of the biggest names in baseball, as well as its leading personalities. In 1947, however, it was Yogi Berra who stole the limelight. Everybody wanted to see this kid, who didn't recognize the legal strike zone and hammered everything that came near the plate out of the ball park, take his swings at the plate. That was all right with Yogi. He enjoyed that well enough. What he couldn't have enjoyed very much was the cruel way some of his own teammates hazed him, poked fun at him, joked about his looks, his clothes, the way he devoured his food. It was like a group of savages, eager to devour its own young.

When Bucky Harris announced in the spring of 1947 that he intended using Berra in the Yankee outfield, rather than as a catcher, the late Rud Rennie, the veteran New York *Herald-Tribune* sportswriter, immediately wrote: "Bucky you can't do this; Berra won't make it. He doesn't even look like a Yankee."

"You're right," Harris agreed. "He doesn't look like one, but he sure enough is going to be one. I'll say this, too. Maybe not this year or next year, but you can bet every by-line you've had on a story that Berra's the Babe Ruth of the future. I wouldn't be at all surprised to see him hit over .300 this season."

The biggest argument against Yogi was that he was a bad-ball hitter. His own personal excuse for this habit that offends the baseball purist was that he could hit anything he could reach, and because of his bad-ball hitting, he became one of the most difficult batters to pitch against.

The second complaint against Berra was that, as a catcher he was clumsy, couldn't throw well, and was unpredictable. One day, while with Newark, he hit his own pitcher in the chest while trying to throw to second base.

The many jokes, remarks, and cruel comparisons made about Yogi's looks was part of baseball's nastiness. Opposing players would tease any opponent to upset and annoy him.

It was all the cruelest kind of hazing, and it might very well have destroyed the confidence of any other youngster, killed any chance of making the baseball big time. Yogi Berra took it in stride. He had been taking that kind of rough personal stuff since he had been a kid playing on the streets and on the sandlots of the Hill in St. Louis.

"I was good enough to play for the Yankees, and that was enough for me," he said.

"Don't any of those cracks bother you?" asked a newspaperman.

It was then that Yogi made his famous retort: "All you have to do in this game is to hit the ball. I never saw nobody hit one with his face."

And Yogi hit that ball. In the opening day game in Washington, with President Harry S. Truman throwing out the first ball, Berra went up against the legendary pitcher Bobo Newsome and banged out 4 hits in his 5 times at bat.

Newsome just looked at the kid and wondered how he did it. Not one of those hits was the result of a ball hurled across the plate and in the strike zone. There was a low outside pitch, a curve right under his chin, a fast ball which should have hit his feet, and a change of pace up around his eyes.

Bobby Brown said of Yogi, "He has the biggest strike zone in baseball. It goes from his ankles to a foot over his head, from his breastbone (Brown is now Dr. Robert Brown) to as far away from the plate as his bat can reach."

The manager of the Detroit Tigers, Steve O'Neill, shook his head in disbelief, watching Yogi batter his pitchers.

"There's no way to pitch to him," he said. "He has no weakness. You can't even waste a pitch on him, when you have two strikes on him. Throw him a bad one and, likely as not, he'll bang it into the stands."

Yogi's work behind the bat and in right field, where Bucky Harris played him, was poor. He still threw curves to second base, trying to nip a runner; and he was something of an uncertainty as an outfielder. Joe ("Ducky") Medwick was with the Yankees that year, and he was assigned to teach Yogi how to judge a ball hit into the outfield, and Yogi surprised Harris with his spirited play in the field. There was always that hesitation, but then the young fellow would go for the ball, fast and furiously. And he was always there to pick the ball out of the air, or field it and send it rocketing back into the infield. The spirit that Yogi showed in the field almost made up for the uncertainty, but once it had the fans groaning as Berra dove for a fly ball and then went crashing into an ailing Joe DiMaggio.

The fans and the sportswriters both yelled for Berra's scalp.

"He's a menace in the outfield," they said and

wrote, but Joe DiMaggio, great player and equally great person that he was, apologized for Yogi.

"I called for the ball, all right," he said, "but Yogi was too anxious to help me. He knows all about that bad heel of mine and figured he was doing something to save me."

"But you called for the ball."

"He thought I was telling him to make the play. And he did try to pull away at the last minute."

Harris continued using Yogi in the outfield, or behind the plate, depending on the condition of Joe DiMaggio, as well as his catching staff. As a catcher, he often had trouble with his pitchers. They didn't always agree with the calls he made from behind the plate. But, with time, and with the coaching he got later on from catcher Bill Dickey, he began to gain more respect for his ability in that key position.

It would take him a little while to learn how to get the ball on a line to second base, but no one was faster or more determined to make the right play at home plate. It was in this year as a Yankee that he pulled off the unassisted double play, tagging out the batter who had bunted the ball, and the runner trying to score from third. He also tagged Cal Hubbard, the home-plate umpire, to make sure he had tagged everybody.

Yogi joined the small list of 19 other catchers who had executed the unassisted double play since 1900. He is the only one in the history of the game to have two such unassisted double plays to his credit—he repeated the first performance some fifteen years later.

Yogi Berra played 83 games in that 1947 season. He went to bat 293 times and collected 82 hits for an average of .280. Among those 82 hits there were 15 doubles, 3 triples, and 11 home runs. His batting average was respectable enough for his first year of hitting against major league pitching. Besides, he batted in 54 runs for the Yankees and scored 41 times himself. Not a bad record for a youngster's first full season in the big time, and if Yogi thought he could do better, Bucky Harris was completely satisfied with his rookie's performance. Yogi's bat undoubtedly was a great help in winning the American League pennant of 1947.

Charley Dressen, who was coaching the Yankees that year, wanted to make Yogi's bat an even more potent weapon than it was. He wanted Yogi to let the bad pitches go, to wait for the good pitch to come his way.

"Don't let them sucker you into swinging at the bad ones," he advised Yogi. "Make them get that good one over the plate. You've got to think when you're up there at the plate. Think about swinging at the good pitch. Think! That's the important thing! You've got to think when you're up there at the plate."

Yogi listened. He was always a good listener. He took his stance in the batter's box and, whatever else he did, he didn't offer even once at the three straight strikes the pitcher hurled across the plate.

He threw his bat away and he was a bewildered young man walking back to the Yankee dugout.

"How do you expect me to hit and think at the same time?" he asked.

The story made the rounds.

Of course Yogi was thinking every minute of the time he went to bat. He couldn't have hit the ball the way he did without thinking. Dressen's effort at improving the hitting of the rookie had just confused him, made him concentrate on thinking instead of on the ball. You've got to concentrate when you're up at bat, and that concentration has to be on the kind of pitch that is coming toward you at better than sixty miles per hour.

There was another time during the season when Yogi's thinking got in the way. It was July in St. Louis. The Yankees were to play the St. Louis Browns. That wasn't the most important thing that day for Yogi. What was more important was that his friends on the Hill had gotten together, collected some money for a number of gifts and arranged to make that game the occasion for a Yogi Berra Night.

Yogi was scared to death for perhaps the first and last time of his life. It wasn't the game that frightened him, or the fact that all his old friends and his family would be in the stands, watching him. What had him all nervous and jittery was the speech he would have to make on the microphone.

"What am I going to say?"

Bobby Brown, his old friend, had the answer.

"I'll write you a speech," he said.

"Thanks," said Yogi, pumping Bobby's hand in deep gratitude. "Make it short, will you?"

He made it short.

"I'm a lucky guy and I'm happy to be with the Yankees. I want to thank everyone for making this night possible."

Yogi worked on those lines all day. He went over them again and again, memorizing every word, and he had Bobby Brown listen to him speak them a dozen

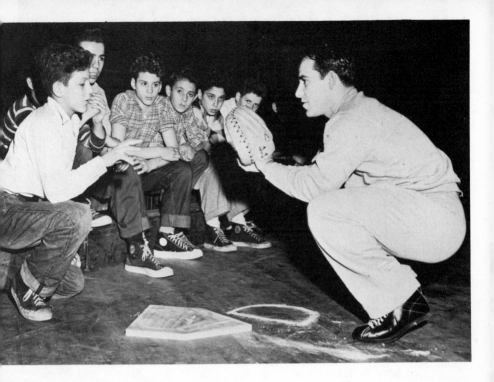

Yogi, who has just found out that he has been named as the Most Valuable Player in the American League for 1951, takes time out to talk baseball with these schoolboys. *(Wide World Photos)*

Two happy ball players—Allie Reynolds, the great Yankee pitcher, and Yogi Berra after beating the Washington Senators in 1952. *(Wide World Photos)*

Crown Prince Akihito stopped off to see a double-header while on his tour of the United States in 1953. Mickey Mantle and Yogi autographed a baseball for him in between games with the St. Louis Browns. Later that year the Yankees went on a barnstorming tour to Japan. *(Wide World Photos)*

Big smiles after the opening World Series win over the Brooklyn Dodgers in 1953. Left to right are: Hank Bauer, Yogi, Billy Martin, and Joe Collins. Bauer had had two hits, Berra homered, Martin tripled with the bases loaded, and Collins homered for the 9–5 win. *(Associated Press Newsphoto)*

Berra does it again. In 1954, he was selected once more as the American League's Most Valuable Player. Here he is with his wife and sons, Larry, 5 (center), and Tim, 3. *(Wide World Photos)*

"The old perfesser," Casey Stengel looks at Yogi's throwing hand following the All-Star game of 1956. Berra had been hit by a foul tip, and Casey, who was the Yankee's manager at the time, was worried. *(Wide World Photos)*

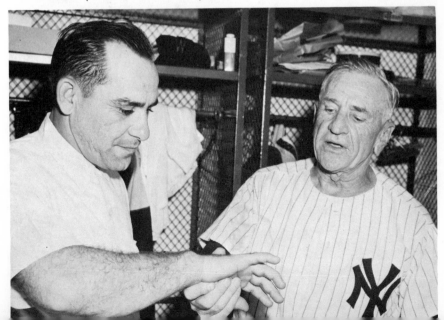

The dugout greeting for Yogi after his second homer of the final game in the 1956 World Series against the Brooklyn Dodgers. This homer gave Yogi a new World Series record of 10 runs batted in. *(Wide World Photos)*

Yogi, in 1959, engages in one of his most important winter activities —reading the fine print in his contract. All he said about it was, "I'm satisfied. I wouldn't have signed it if I wasn't." *(Wide World Photos)*

times and more. He was almost at ease when the Yogi Berra Night was climaxed with the gift of a brand new Nash sedan. He strode up to the plate to accept the car and to make his memorized speech. That's when it happened. The mike got in the way. It was like having a gun pointed at his head.

He hemmed and he hawed, then he managed to get the first of the two sentences Bobby Brown had written for him into that dread microphone.

"I'm a lucky guy and I'm happy to be with the Yankees."

He hesitated. That second sentence seemed to have gotten away from him.

Finally, he blurted into that live instrument, for the whole world to hear and remember, "And I want to thank everyone for making this night necessary!"

Necessary!?

That was Yogi. He knew how to turn a phrase.

Chapter 9

World Series time is a time of tension even for the most seasoned of major league stars. Yogi Berra was only twenty-two and had played only one year in the big leagues. He could well be expected to have the World Series jitters; and he did. But it wasn't because he was going to be participating in the annual major classic for the baseball championship of the world; it was because Bucky Harris had told him that he would be the Yankees' starting catcher in this year's battle against the Yankees' bitter rival, the Brooklyn Dodgers.

He was also jittery because he knew it takes more than one season to make a top backstop. Besides, Yogi had been shifted in and out of the catcher's position, as Bucky Harris kept putting him into right field, just to have his bat in the line-up. Young Berra was fast around the plate, but his throwing to the bases, to cut down attempted steals, was still far from accurate. And the Brooklyn Dodgers, who had won the National League pennant, had its full quota of great base stealers. There was Pistol Pete Reiser and Pee

Wee Reese, and especially that great base runner, Jackie Robinson.

"How are you going to stop them from running?" the sportswriters queried.

"Jackie Robinson never stole a base on me when he was playing for Montreal," said Yogi, trying to build up his courage with recollections of the days both he and Jackie played in the International League.

But Yogi was worried. He had plenty of reason to worry. And the worry affected his hitting.

In the first two games of the Series, both Jackie Robinson and Pee Wee Reese stole bases on Yogi. Burt Shotton, manager of the Dodgers, had made it public enough that his boys would run on Yogi, and they did. What was even worse, at least for Bucky Harris' strategy, was that Yogi was in a fearsome batting slump in those two initial games of the classic. Eight times, in those two games, Yogi walked up to the plate, and all he could do was collect a single base on balls. Still, there were two spectacular moments for Yogi in that World Series, one of which he would have liked to forget.

He was catching Bill Bevens in the fourth game and Bevens was pitching the game of his life, though he was wild. He kept missing the plate and walking batters. He was in trouble almost every inning, but with two out in the ninth and Al Gionfriddo running for Carl Furillo (who had walked) on first base, Bevens had not allowed a single base hit. He was on the verge of pitching the first no-hit game in World Series history.

But, with Pete Reiser up at the plate, and Bevens

73

pitching carefully and deliberately, perhaps too deliberately, little Al Gionfriddo took off for second.

Gionfriddo had a good jump on the pitcher, the pitch was low. Berra whipped the ball to second base, to Phil Rizzuto; the throw was high and Phil had to leap high in the air, then come down with the ball— too late! Gionfriddo was safe and the tag which would have made it three out for the Dodgers and the first no-hitter in the World Series, was never made.

It is true that Bevens had failed to keep Gionfriddo close to first, that he had taken too much time in his wind-up, that all his concentration had been on Pete Reiser and the desire to make him the final out of the game; but Yogi never forgave himself for that high throw.

"I should have got him."

Pete Reiser walked, and Cookie Lavagetto took care of history and that potential no-hitter by banging a fast ball on a line to the right-field fence. It was a wallop that was good enough for a two-bagger, two Dodger runs, the ball game, and the end of a history-making dream.

Both Bevens and Yogi walked slowly back to their clubhouse, tears in their eyes.

There was, however, one really happy moment in that fall classic for Yogi Berra; and that moment, too, made baseball history.

It was the third game of the Series. Bucky Harris had pulled Yogi out of the line-up. He had Sherman Lollar catching in what proved to be the wildest set-to in the classic.

Both teams were hitting the ball. The score was 9–7 in the seventh inning. Harris signaled Yogi to get up from the bench. He needed runs. He needed a pinch hitter. Maybe, he thought, Yogi could get a hit. Start something. Get the team moving.

Ralph Branca was pitching. Branca wasn't going to give Yogi Berra anything good to hit. The difficulty was that when Yogi was in a hitting mood there was nothing that wasn't good enough for him to swing at.

The Dodger pitcher took his wind-up, hurled the ball toward the plate. It may have been a little high, a little low, a bit inside or a bit outside; Branca doesn't remember. What he does remember, and what Yogi will never forget, is that Berra took his full swing and, with that powerful snap of his wrists, met the ball, and sent it screaming out of the ball park for a home run. It was the first time in the history of the classic that anyone had come to bat to bang out a pinch-hit home run.

It was a great moment for the youngster. He was destined to play in more World Series games than Babe Ruth, Lou Gehrig, Joe DiMaggio—in fact, he holds the record for participating in more World Series games than any other player in the game's history—but that first Series and his first entry into the record-makers' books unquestionably contributed much to the development that made him one of the greatest of all catchers in the story of baseball.

Yogi came home to St. Louis a hero. He also came home with a check for $5,830, his share of the World Series money. It was the biggest check he had ever held, and it was $830 more than his salary as a regular Yankee for 1947. He kept it long enough to show everyone in the family that baseball was not a bum's game; then put it into the bank. Yogi was not one of those fellows who tossed money around as soon as he got it. He had come through some hard times and knew the value of the dollar. He would use his dollars wisely.

It was during the winter between the Series and 1948 spring training that Yogi met Carmen Short, the pretty young girl who was to become his wife. It wasn't easy, meeting her. Even at the age of twenty-two, Yogi was still shy when it came to talking to girls.

"She wasn't the first girl I went out with," he said. "She was the third."

He saw her for the first time while she was waiting on tables in a restaurant, and he was immediately smitten. But how to meet her? How to ask her out on a date? Yogi was as ignorant of such techniques as he was ignorant of solid geometry.

It was Julius "Biggie" Garagnini, who owned the restaurant, who saw the stars come into Yogi's eyes and was good enough to introduce his beautiful wait-ress to the love-struck, shy baseball star.

As luck would have it, they fell in love, and it was a happy winter for them in St. Louis. Usually along with Joey Garagiola and his friend Audrie Ross, they went to the movies, saw a basketball game or a hockey game. The romance flourished, but it took Yogi more than six months to propose marriage; and then, he didn't do it in the age-old manner.

He asked Carmen to dinner with his family and when they were all seated at the table, as the pretty young girl turned her head to talk to brother An-thony, Yogi slipped a box with a diamond ring in it on to Carmen's plate.

76

Carmen knew what was in that box. Her face lit up. She took out the ring. She put it on her finger.

Yogi never did actually ask her to marry him, and Carmen never did actually say she would. It was all understood. For once, Yogi's difficulties with the English language didn't get in the way. Nor did his shyness.

They were married the winter of 1948, in St. Ambrose Church, where his mother and father had been married. Pete Reiser of the Dodgers was at the wedding. So were Ducky Medwick, Lonnie Frey, and a host of other ballplayers. Joe Garagiola was his best man. (Yogi would be best man at Joe's wedding the next year.) It was to develop into one of the happiest marriages in or out of baseball.

"How come you married a girl named 'Short'?" Yogi was once asked by the St. Louis broadcaster, Harry Caray. "That's not an Italian name."

"My mother likes her," said Yogi, which seemed like an answer out of left field.

His answer to the next query was a bit wilder, for anyone who knew Yogi.

"How do the girls on the Hill feel about your marrying an outsider?"

"They had their chance!" said Yogi.

And that was that, from a fellow who had confided to Joe DiMaggio, once, "The girls won't bother with me. I guess I'm just too ugly for dates."

Beauty, as Carmen was called, and the beast, as Yogi was so often called, did all right. They were in love, and love, blind or not, kept them together.

As for the "beast," it is interesting to note that The National Association of Women Artists voted, in

77

1950, Yogi the man with the "most stimulating face" in America. Maybe Carmen saw a lot more in Yogi than did the ballplayers, the sportswriters, the fans, and even Yogi himself.

Chapter 10

The New York Yankees, champions of the baseball world in 1947, didn't do too well in 1948. There seemed to be a general letdown, both in spirit and performance. Except for the ailing Joe DiMaggio and the second-year Yogi Berra, the club certainly didn't play up to its potential—and Yogi still had a way to go before he could be recognized as a full-fledged baseball star.

He had just turned twenty-three at the beginning of the season, and there was much for him to learn. He continued to have his troubles as the first-string catcher. His work behind the plate and his throwing were still erratic, but he continued his fine and timely work with the bat, giving the Yankees the threat of the long ball which could turn a ball game around.

During a stretch of 21 games in that 1948 season, Yogi connected for 34 hits in 85 times at bat for an even .400 average. He wound up the year with a most respectable average of .305, hammering 143 hits off his opposing pitchers. Twenty-four of those hits were doubles, 10 triples and 14 home runs. He crossed the plate to score exactly 70 runs and batted in 98 more for the Yankee club.

"It should have been 100," said Yogi, if the rains hadn't washed out the game and the home run he hit off the Detroit Tigers' Dizzy Trout, with a man on base.

Perhaps the most important statistic for Yogi that year, however, was the average of the runs he batted in per time at bat. Red Patterson of the Yankees' publicity staff, who worked out those statistics, showed that Yogi was sixth in the league in that crucial area of the game. It indicated that Yogi hit best when it counted, when there were men on base, when the runs needed to win a game could be scored. He used this vital baseball statistic in his first salary battle with the New York front office.

The Yankees had given Yogi a fairly decent raise in his salary for the 1948 season. He had been jumped from $5,000 to $8,500. George Weiss, who was then the top man in the New York front office, offered Yogi another $1,500 for 1949. That would have brought his salary up to $10,000.

Yogi thought, and not without good reason, that his bat in the Yankee line-up was worth a lot more.

"I'm asking for $15,000," he said, and he sent his contract, unsigned, back to Weiss.

The first of the long series of salary hassles between Berra and the front office was on.

Yogi knew what he was worth to the Yankee organization, but George Weiss was not easily moved when it came to shelling out money for the New York club. Besides, he had a pretty good argument for his position, an argument with which Yogi Berra could do very little.

"You're asking me to practically double your salary," he said. "I know you had a pretty good season last year, but one good season doesn't entitle you to that kind of tremendous increase in your contract. You can't expect to get the salary the older players, the men who have had a good number of good seasons over a good number of years. You've just begun. One season doesn't make a ballplayer.

"We're ready to pay you what you're worth," continued George Weiss, than whom there was no one wiser in the game of bargaining with baseball men. "Prove to us you're worth $15,000 and you'll get it. We're prepared to pay a man what he earns."

Yogi chalked that remark down in his memory book. He would use it, and the Yankees would pay him a whole lot more than $15,000 per season, in due time.

Meanwhile, Yogi settled for a salary of $12,000, which wasn't a bad salary for the young ballplayer, considering his 1948 performance. There was no doubt about what he could do with his bat. His fielding, and particularly his play behind the plate, still raised a mighty big question mark about his baseball future. After all a ballplayer has to be a good glove man, as well as a top batter, to stay in the big leagues.

It was Yogi's glove that was the Yankees' main concern. It would be Yogi's concern, especially when Casey Stengel, the new man in the managerial post in New York in 1949, declared that Tommy Henrich would play right field for the club.

"If Yogi Berra plays," he said, "it'll have to be behind the plate."

"If he plays . . ."

The sportswriters picked up that phrase.

"Berra Doubtful," in one form or another, headed the sports columns that spring of 1949, with the Yankees reporting for spring training in St. Petersburg, Florida.

"Berra has got to be a catcher if we're going to use him," said Casey.

The pressure was on.

But Stengel realized that Berra needed coaching if he expected him to develop into a top-flight catcher. He needed help, expert help, and he provided it for the young ballplayer. He got hold of Bill Dickey, who had retired from the game and was enjoying a life of leisure, and talked him into donning his baseball uniform once more. Dickey was going to join the Yankee staff as a coach. His main job, however, was to turn Yogi Berra into a first-rate catcher for the Yankees.

Dickey did more than that. He helped develop young Berra into one of the greatest catchers in the history of the diamond. He took Berra in hand early in spring training for the 1949 season. He was a smart teacher. Not only did he work on Yogi's faults as a catcher, he concentrated as well on building up the confidence of the young ballplayer. No matter how much natural talent a man has, if he lacks confidence, none of that talent is going to be realized.

Casey was going to help along these lines, too.

"Next to Joe DiMaggio," he said, "Yogi Berra is the best player of them all."

Being next to Joe DiMaggio on the totem pole was

enough to inspire any ballplayer, young or old, to great feats on the diamond.

"Get up close to the batter," said Bill Dickey to his student, who showed a ready, even an eager willingness to learn. "You've got two feet there you can close up. Don't be afraid of tipping the bat. You've plenty of room."

Yogi followed instructions. He learned that getting up closer to the batter also protected him from a lot of injuries due to foul tips. The ball sliced by him, instead of hitting his hands, his arms, his body.

"Get that close to the batter, and you can step right over home plate and whip the ball to second base. That extra split second will cut the runner down for you."

Yogi listened and learned.

"Bill Dickey learned me all his experience," Yogi would say, later, murdering the King's English, as always, in the process.

"You've been throwing the ball off-balance," said Dickey. "That's why your throw to second base is off the mark. You're sailing the ball. Now, when you get ready to throw, don't bring your hand all the way back of your head, throw the ball right off your ear and use plenty of wrist action. Step forward with your throw. Make sure your feet are balanced and don't worry about the guy at bat."

Hour after hour, day in and day out, Bill Dickey picked Yogi's faults apart, showed him the correct way to do things behind the plate, and day in and day out Yogi practiced under the eyes of his great mentor.

It was amazing to both Dickey and Casey Stengel that Yogi improved almost at once.

He had to learn how to judge the foul ball that goes straight up, anywhere around the plate. The ball is sure to come down some time, but what were the winds going to do with it? Blow it in front of you? Behind you? And catching a foul ball at the plate very often means the difference between a game won and a game lost.

There is also the problem of playing the ball thrown in from the outfield to cut down the runner going from third base to home on a sacrifice fly. The catcher has to judge how that ball is coming to him. Does he have time to wait for it, or does he have to run up the line to get it? And on which side of the plate is it coming? You have to do all that split-second thinking and judging with one eye on the runner coming in from third.

Bill Dickey was patient with Yogi, but he was also surprised at the humility of the young fellow, as well as the quickness with which he learned.

"Catch the ball first," said Dickey. "Adjust your grip. Then throw it.

"Another thing to remember," Dickey continued. "The catcher is the only player who faces the entire field of play. So you have to watch and move your players around for each type of hitter. You're like a quarterback. You have to be alert and wide awake all the time."

Every day in spring training, for at least two hours, Bill Dickey delivered his instructions and Yogi followed them, practicing, practicing, and practicing again all the fine points his teacher insisted on. And it paid off, for both the Yankees and Yogi.

"Give him two years," said the all-time great

catcher of the Yankees, Bill Dickey, "and he'll be the greatest catcher in the American League, by a long shot."

Bill Dickey was right.

Right from the start of the 1949 season, Berra became a terror behind the plate as he cut down runner after runner with clean accurate bulletlike throws. He caught almost everything that was popped up around home plate. And like a big cat he pounced on that bunt and pegged it to first, so fast that bunting became a hazardous play for the Yankee's opposing batsmen.

Yogi was a different ballplayer in 1949. He played his position with more skill and consistency and with increasing confidence. And the skill and accuracy rubbed off on the Yankee pitching staff. Pitchers no longer feared the days they would have to have Yogi as the backstop on their pitching assignments; they welcomed them.

For years to come Yogi was going to be considered the top catcher in baseball. "Berra," said Casey Stengel, "is why our pitchers have been doing so good. The kid's been great in the close ones, and the way he's been handling those pitchers. There's nobody that has the pitcher's confidence like Mr. Berra. Nobody's running on him, and they better not. The way he's throwing, even Ty Cobb couldn't steal on him now."

Maybe Casey meant every word he said, or maybe he was just saying it all for Yogi's morale. In either case, the young ballplayer ate it up, and he was the better Yankee for it all.

There were some bad moments for Yogi in that 1949 season. Early in May, he got hit in the head by an errant throw during infield practice. He was unconscious when they carried him off the field and rushed him to the hospital. Doctors stitched a half-inch gash above his right eye, but the X rays of his head proved negative.

The newspaper writers couldn't miss this opportunity to gibe at the good-natured kid from St. Louis.

"X rays of Yogi's head showed nothing."

Early in August, Yogi, who managed to get hurt more than most ballplayers, was injured again; and this time the injury was considerably more serious.

It happened during one of those games in which the opposing pitchers try to bean ball their opposing batters. Once a pitcher aims the ball at the opposing batters, there usually follows retaliation and then a free-for-all. Someone is bound to get hurt, sometimes badly. In this particular game, between the St. Louis Browns and the New York Yankees, three New York players were hit.

The first victim was Yogi. Dick Starr hit him on his left thumb. Karl Drews, the relief pitcher, hit Henrich on his right elbow. He also hit Jerry Coleman, but not as seriously.

Both Henrich and Yogi were rushed to Lenox Hill Hospital. X rays showed Tommy ("Old Reliable") Henrich had suffered only a bad bruise. This meant he would have to miss a couple of times at bat for a few days. Yogi's thumb was fractured. He couldn't swing a bat properly, and he was scheduled to be out of the game for at least three weeks.

Casey Stengel didn't believe this; or he pretended not to believe it. Maybe it was his way of needling Yogi back into the line-up. The Yankees had had a comfortable lead in first place on July 4, but with Yogi out of the batting box, the Boston Red Sox were coming up fast. The situation had Casey worried.

"This is Mr. Berra," he would say to a newspaperman, as if Yogi were new to the club.

"He doesn't do any work around here," Casey would say. "He says he's got some kind of pain that's bothering him."

Casey had real affection for the young fellow. Sometimes he was even inclined to play the father with him. It could very well have been that he didn't want Yogi to baby his injury; or that Casey didn't understand the full extent of it.

Anyway, he had Yogi suit up every day, run around the ball park, play the outfield during batting practice. He wouldn't even let Yogi break away, injury and all, to St. Louis, where Carmen had decided to stay until the baby she and Yogi were expecting arrived. Of course, Casey knew that that baby wasn't due till September, and he wanted Yogi near him all the time, if only to keep him in playing shape for when that broken thumb had healed.

It wasn't until September 7, that Yogi finally saw action again. He had been out for more than a month. He inserted two pieces of sponge in his glove, to protect the thumb which was still quite sore, but he did well enough behind the plate that day, pegging the ball twice to second to nip the two Red Sox who tried to steal a base on him. His bat, even after he unwound all the tape on his sore thumb, might have been left in the rack for all the good it did. He went 0 for 3, and a severe pain shot through his arm every time he so much as made contact with the ball.

It took a while, but the pain finally went, much to Casey's relief. He didn't want his prize catcher hurt, but those fighting Boston Red Sox had not only caught up with the Yankees, they were a full game ahead, with only two games left on the schedule. Those games were with the New York club, and a victory in just one of them would have given them the flag.

They couldn't do it. The Yankees won both games and wound up with 97 wins against 57 losses, just a game on each side of the ledger better than the Red Sox could do.

Yogi's average dropped a bit in those last days of the 1949 season. But he finished with the respectable average of .277, with 115 hits, 20 of them doubles, 2 triples, and 20 home runs. He scored 59 runs in 116 games and banged in 91. If his batting average was below par, his average for getting those runs in when they counted was still high, among the highest in the league.

The first year that Yogi Berra was elected to the American League All-Star team was 1949. He was to be elected to that all-star squad every year thereafter, as long as he was an active player.

Unhappily, for some reason Yogi can't explain, he never played well in the inter-league games, whether they were all-star or the classic World Series. With a few exceptional years, his bat was all but dead when he faced National League pitching.

This was certainly true in the 1949 World Series. The Yankees made a romp of it over the Brooklyn Dodgers. They took four of five games to win the World Championship again. Yogi did a good job behind the plate, but all he could get with his bat was 1 hit in 16 times at bat. It is worth noting, however, that that one hit batted in a run for New York.

If Yogi was disturbed by his performance at bat, he certainly gave no evidence of it. On the contrary, he was the happiest of baseball players. The Yankees had won, he went home $5,665.54 richer (his share of the World Series prize money) and what was most important to the young fellow, he had proven to the baseball world that he was a big league catcher, one of its best, one who had been voted into the All-Star game and caught the last six innings of it.

If anybody was responsible for this critical change in Yogi's play, the change which would eventually land him in baseball's Hall of Fame, it was Bill Dickey, with an assist from that wisest of old-timers, Casey Stengel.

Yogi was no longer just a ballplayer when he returned to St. Louis; he was a celebrity, though it would have been hard to guess it, seeing him pal around with his old friends in restaurants and bars. He would always remain a simple and honest fellow, which is probably why he has remained a favorite over the years.

Certainly, no one could guess, those winter days in St. Louis, how far this young man from the Hill was still to travel, or how great his fame would become.

Chapter 11

During the winter of 1949 Yogi was pleased to read that the Baseball Writers Association, in its annual election of the Most Valuable Player in the American League for the season just concluded, had voted him fifteenth place. To have gotten any ballots at all in that selection was honor enough. To have been placed as high as fifteenth in the standing set Yogi's mind to some quick calculations.

He knew, as well as did everyone else in the game, that he had overcome his major weaknesses as a catcher, and that his hitting was something the Yankees appreciated considerably. He also recalled the famous words of George Weiss, the big front-office man of the New York club.

"We're prepared to pay a man what he earns."

"I'm going to ask for $22,000," he said to Carmen. He thought for a moment. "I'll take $18,000, but that's rock bottom."

Carmen never interfered with her husband's baseball business, but she could calculate as quickly as Yogi.

"That's a $10,000 raise you're asking for."

"Weiss said he'd pay me what I was worth," said Yogi. "I swear to the Lord that I won't take less than . . . $18,000!"

Yogi, according to Carmen, never broke a vow to the Lord. Weiss, of course, wasn't aware of this special characteristic of his star catcher, but even if he had been, he would probably have told Yogi that he had no right to make any arrangements of that kind with the Almighty before consulting with the Yankee front office.

In any case, he sent Yogi his contract for 1950, as usual at the last minute, just before the legal deadline of January 1, and there was nothing like a $22,000 salary in it. It wasn't a bad contract. It called for a $4,000 raise and $16,000 for the year, but it was nowhere near the $22,000 Yogi had in mind, or the $18,000 deal Yogi had made with the Lord.

He mailed the contract back to Weiss, and told him what he wanted. Weiss, generally a cool operator in money matters, momentarily lost his control.

"The kid wants to become the richest player in baseball in the shortest possible time!"

The sportswriters make as much as they can of any kind of news that comes along between the baseball seasons, and Yogi's salary disputes were going to make news for a good number of years.

"You sent back your contract?" asked one of the St. Louis sports columnists.

"Yeah," said Yogi, in his noncommittal manner.

"What did they offer you?"

Yogi wasn't going to tell him. There is a sort of secrecy about baseball players' salaries.

"I don't know," he said.

91

The sportswriter did a double take.

"How come you don't know? Didn't you read the contract?"

Yogi thought that he was being asked a funny kind of question. He played along with it.

"Nope," he said. "I didn't read it."

Needless to say, this became another much publicized story in the collection of stories that circulated around in the sports world, all to indicate that Yogi was some sort of zany character, which of course, as baseball would learn, he was not.

The story didn't sit well with Weiss, as might have been expected, but with spring training in St. Petersburg already under way, the front office man finally called Yogi on the phone.

"You're not doing yourself or the club any good in St. Louis," he said. "Take a plane down here and let's talk it over."

"Who'll pay for the fare, if I don't sign?" asked Yogi, in the manner of business dealing which had become part of his character.

The New York organization paid the fare, but the meeting between Weiss and Yogi was far from cordial. They were both hard bargainers, and at one moment, after two hours of mounting tempers, they were actually yelling at each other.

"Let me see Dan Topping or Del Webb!" shouted Yogi. Topping and Webb were the owners of the New York club. "I can't talk to you any more!"

But Topping and Webb were not available for Yogi, and he was mad enough to start packing to go back to St. Louis. He wasn't breaking his word to the Lord for George Weiss, the Yankees, or anybody else.

"You'd think I was a flop last year," he snapped. "I had a very good year!" he bellowed, "in case nobody else told you!"

It was old Casey Stengel who managed to keep him down in St. Petersburg, and it was Casey who convinced George Weiss that Yogi had earned the right to an $18,000 salary. Neither Casey nor Weiss would regret the deal.

Nineteen-fifty was a great year for the twenty-five-year-old Yogi Berra. He started off with a rush. He got 3 hits in the opening game of the season. He got a home run and 3 singles in 5 times at bat in the first game at Yankee Stadium. In the first two weeks of the season Yogi hammered the ball to all parts of Yankee Stadium, and his batting average climbed over .400.

"The way you're going," the newspaper reporters said, "you'll be right there on top with the leading hitters."

Yogi shook the reporters off.

"I'm a bad-ball hitter. Bad-ball hitters aren't supposed to hit for high batting averages."

But Yogi's bat was a tremendous factor in the Yankee line-up, as the Bronx Bombers went on to cool off the strong Red Sox to win the pennant. It was Yogi's best year as a Yankee. He played in nearly every game . . . 151 to be exact, a record for a Yankee catcher. He slammed out 192 hits—30 doubles, 6 triples, and 28 home runs. He scored 116 times and batted in 124 runs.

In the World Series the Yankees faced the powerful Philadelphia Phillies. The Phillies, the same club which leaped from sixth place in 1948 to third in '49 had suffered severely in the run for the pennant. Curt Simmons, the team's twenty-one-year-old pitching ace, was called into military service, and two other young pitching aces, Bob Miller and Bubba Church, were side-lined with injuries. The able-bodied youngsters who made up the Phillies line-up tried so hard against the Yankees that they tightened up and failed to hit in the clinches.

The first game saw Vic Raschi of the Yankees and Jim Konstanty locked in a great pitchers' battle. Raschi was so good that only three Phillies reached first base, and he was in trouble in only one inning, the fifth, when Jones and Andy Seminick bunched two hits. But they were left stranded when Yogi made a great throw to get Jones as he tore down to third base in an attempt at a double steal. The Yankees won the game in the fourth inning when Bobby Brown slashed a double down the left-field line, and scored when Jerry Coleman sent him home with a long sacrifice fly for a 1–0 win.

In the second game, Allie Reynolds, the Yankee ace, faced Robin Roberts, and the two great pitchers blasted the ball past the hitters in another marvelous duel of great pitching. Roberts lost the game in the tenth inning, when Joe DiMaggio, after popping up six straight times, drove the ball out of the park. It was DiMaggio's first 1950 Series hit, and it won the game for the Yankees, 2–1.

Both managers nominated southpaw pitchers for the third game of the Series. Stengel called on Eddie Lopat, and Eddie Sawyer of the Phils selected Ken Heintzelman. Ken did pitch beautifully for eight innings, giving up but four hits to the slugging Yanks,

94

including a double by Berra, but with two outs in the eighth inning, Heintzelman blew up and gave up three walks in succession to Joe Coleman, Berra, and DiMaggio.

Bobby Brown then slashed a grounder down the third base line that Granny Hamner kicked around, and Coleman scored the tying run. Then the Yanks went on to blast the ball in the ninth inning to score the winning run and the third straight Series game, 3–2.

The Yankees started their twenty-one-year-old pitching ace, Whitey Ford, in an attempt to sweep the series in four games, and Whitey pitched the game of his life. He held the Phillies scoreless until the ninth inning, and with the help of some tremendous hitting by his battery-mate, Yogi Berra, who drove out a single, double, and home run, Whitey went down to the very last out, but then wilted. Casey Stengel called on Allie Reynolds to get the last out when the Phils had the bases full. Allie struck out pinch hitter Stan Lopata to wrap up the series for the Yankees in four straight games.

The fans had made Yogi Berra their choice as the Number One catcher in the American League for the 1950 All-Star game. It is the fans who elect the first eight players in the line-up for this mid-season classic. The manager of each competing club selects the pitcher. Yogi did a professional job behind the plate in the game which was played in Chicago's Comiskey Park that year. But, true to form, he did nothing with his bat. Why, except for very few of the classics—All-Star or World Series—Yogi's bat might just as well have been left in the locker is something Berra has never been able to explain, or even understand.

"Maybe I tighten up," he said.

Yogi's clutch hitting, along with his great batting average, his 28 home runs, and his exceptional play behind the plate, made him a strong candidate for the Most Valuable Player in the American League Award that year of 1950. And he polled a strong vote. Three of the sportswriters put him in first place; but Billy Goodman, who won the batting crown that season, got four first-place votes; and little Phil Rizzuto, who had his greatest year at shortstop for the Yankees in 1950, was voted first place by sixteen of the sportswriters.

That year Phil Rizzuto got that MVP Award all the way with 284 points. Billy Goodman was second with 180 points. Yogi was third with 146—a remarkable vote of recognition for a fellow who had played for only four years in the big leagues. It told Yogi, just in case he didn't know it, that, with the possible exception of two other men, he was the best baseball player in his league.

Bill Dickey's prediction had come true. It had come true even earlier than the great star had predicted.

"Give him two years," he had said, "and he'll be the greatest catcher in the American League, by a long shot."

Bill Dickey had been not only a great ballplayer, he had become a prophet. And no one in the Yankee organization could have been more pleased than Casey Stengel and George Weiss; that is, nobody could have been more pleased than these two fine gentlemen until it came to sign up Yogi for the 1951 season.

Chapter 12

The year 1951 was memorable in baseball. This was the unforgettable year in which Bobby Thomson of the New York Giants hit a three-run homer off Dodger pitcher Ralph Branca in the bottom of the ninth inning to win the third play-off game for the Giants. This was a win that gave the Giants the pennant after the Dodgers had had a seemingly insurmountable lead of thirteen-and-a-half games at mid-August.

It was also the year that saw Joe DiMaggio hang up his glove, his bat, and his spikes to retire from one of the most remarkable careers in the story of baseball. It was the end of an era for the New York Yankees; perhaps the beginning of a new one.

DiMaggio was to the Yankees what Babe Ruth had been in an earlier era. He was the most graceful ballplayer, most dangerous clutch hitter, and finally, in 1955, was voted the "greatest living ballplayer"—and at the same time was voted into Baseball's Hall of Fame.

Nineteen fifty-one was also the year that Mickey Mantle powered his way into the starting line-up at age nineteen, and it was the year in which Yogi Berra was voted the Most Valuable Player in the American League.

With DiMaggio playing out the year in one of his worst batting slumps, it was Yogi Berra who became the mainstay of the Yankee attack. In September, as the team fought savagely for the pennant, Yogi was inserted into the number four spot in the batting order, but that didn't work. Perhaps it was the pressure of taking over Joe DiMaggio's clean-up batting position. Perhaps it was Yogi's preoccupation with Carmen and the new baby the Berras were expecting.

"Yogi has a bad year every time I'm going to have a baby," said Carmen.

Nevertheless, and despite his personal worries, Yogi and the Yankees won the pennant again, and there was once again a subway series with the Yankees and the New York Giants.

It had been fourteen years since these two neighboring rivals had met in the fall classic, and New York was the most excited city in the world as the teams prepared to do battle.

In the opening game of the series, the Giants, still red-hot, won behind the magnificent pitching of Dave Koslo, who outpitched Allie Reynolds. Koslo allowed the slugging Yanks just 6 hits, while the Giant hitters, Alvin Dark and Monte Irvin, pounded Reynolds for 10 solid hits to win the opener.

The Yankees struck back in the second game as Eddie Lopat outpitched Larry Jansen, and the Yanks evened the series to win 3–1. But the victory was a costly one for the Yankees as Mickey Mantle, the Yankees great rookie star, tripped and fell while chasing a Willie Mays fly ball in center field. Mickey lay limp and motionless as DiMaggio and trainer Gus Mauch ran out to help him. He was carried off the field, and that was the end of the series for him.

Jim Hearn out-dueled Vic Raschi in the third game as the Giants pounded out 6 runs to win 6–2. In the fourth game Allie Reynolds bounced back to defeat Sal Maglie of the Giants as Yogi and Joe DiMaggio supplied the hitting power. The Yanks won 6–2. DiMaggio, hitless up to this game, clinched the victory for the Yankees by slamming a Maglie pitch over the fence with Berra on base.

The fifth game was a walk-away as the Yankees bombed the Giants for a 13–1 victory. Yogi, Phil Rizzuto, Joe DiMaggio, and Bobby Brown hit solid base hits to drive four Giant pitchers to cover.

The Yankees won the sixth and final game of the series, but the score was 4–3 and the finish was a torrid one. Raschi, hard-pressed all the way, was replaced by Johnny Sain who pitched well until the ninth inning, when the Giants scored twice and had two men on base. Sal Yvars, pinch-hitting for Hank Thompson, hit what looked like a sure double, but Hank Bauer in right field for the Bronx Bombers dove for the ball and caught it just before it hit the turf. As Bauer made the final, heroic catch, Yogi tossed his glove skyward, yanked his mask off and dashed out to congratulate Raschi. He jumped on Vic's back for joy, and the rest of the Yankees, led by Joe DiMaggio, Rizzuto, Gene Woodling, and Hank Bauer, carried both Berra and the grinning, happy Raschi into the dressing room for one of the happiest, wildest Yankee celebrations of all time.

Yogi emerged from the World Series as one of the Yankee stars. His work behind the plate was flawless. He handled his pitchers with skill and confidence, and his big bat blasted out 6 hits. They no longer joked and made fun of the "Kid from St. Louis," for he was now one of baseball's great stars.

There were other moments in that year of 1951 that Yogi would remember for a long time. There was the day, September 28, with the Yankees battling the Red Sox, the Indians, and the White Sox for first place. Allie Reynolds pitched his second no-hit game, this time against the Red Sox. Yogi would never forget that moment. With two out in the ninth, Ted Williams, one of the greatest hitters of all time, popped the ball up behind the plate—and Yogi dropped it. He would have liked to drop out of the Yankee Stadium forever at that moment.

"It was the worst moment I ever had in baseball," Yogi said later.

But, luckily, as Yogi said, Williams popped it up again, right over Yogi's head.

"What if I drop this one!" thought Yogi, and he must have said a thousand Hail Marys waiting for that ball to come down.

It came down. Yogi stuck out his mitt and grabbed the ball. The game was over. Allie Reynolds had his no-hitter, and Yogi scarcely had the strength left to move to his pitcher, give him that big congratulations hug.

Then there was the night in St. Louis when Yogi nearly got himself tossed out of the Yankee line-up and out of the game for an extended period, which would have done neither him nor his club any good.

With the bases full, Ed Hurley, the umpire, called a fourth ball on the Yankee pitcher, Vic Raschi.

Yogi was certain it was a strike, right over the heart of the plate, and that the batter should have been called out. He threw off his mask, and he threw his 200 pounds at the umpire. The umpire pushed back. Yogi grabbed the umpire's arm, ready to let him have his fist; and he would have done it if Casey Stengel hadn't moved out of the dugout fast to intervene. Yogi was thrown out of the game, of course, but it took a lot of pushing and shoving by Casey to get him off the field.

It was Casey, the diplomat, who also got Yogi to apologize to Hurley after the game, and after Yogi had cooled down a bit.

Casey's strategy worked, as it almost always did. Yogi could very easily have been suspended from baseball for at least ten days. The cost to the Yankee pennant drive would have been immeasurable. As it turned out, Hurley, like everyone else in and around baseball, was fond of Yogi. His report to the president of the league was very much on the mild side. Yogi got off easy, with a $100 fine.

A happier moment for the Yankee catcher was the night he appeared on TV with Milton Berle, the Uncle Miltie who had been dubbed "Mr. Television." It was one of the most hilarious TV programs of the year as Berle and Berra joked back and forth with each other.

It was Yogi's love for comic books which got him an offer of a program of his own on TV. He was to do an imitation of Fiorello H. LaGuardia, the once turbulent mayor of New York who had read the newspaper comic sections for the benefit of all the children of the city, during a newspaper strike. The front offce of the Yankees, however, frowned on the deal.

"It lacks dignity," they said.

Dignity?

This was a new word in Yogi's vocabulary. It seemed to indicate that he would have to lose some of that "hail, fellow, well met" attitude he had had back on the Hill in St. Louis, and which he carried with him wherever he went. It seemed to mean that he would have to cut out his down-to-earth honest way of talking, saying just exactly what he meant. It seemed to demand that he be more careful about choosing his companions, how he ate, and what he wore.

Yogi hadn't even worn a tie when he reported for the first time to the New York Yankees.

"Ties choke my throat," he said.

He still didn't wear ties. He would never give up his love for hot dogs and hamburgers. Back in St. Louis, he would continue to sit at the bar or in restaurants with his old pals from the Hill, as if he had never left that Little Italy of his boyhood. There was nothing pretentious about Yogi and there never would be. If he was nothing else, he was Mr. Ordinary Citizen: no airs, straight-spoken, and always completely and utterly honest.

The Yankee front office said that now that he was a big star, maybe the biggest star on the New York roster, he would have to walk, talk, eat, think, behave as a man of dignity behaves.

Yogi would give it a try.

It wouldn't work.

Chapter 13

Yogi Berra had been voted the Most Valuable Player in the American League for 1951. For the Yankees, even before the spring training sessions had got under way, it was recognized that Yogi was going to be the most valuable, the key player for the New York organization in 1952.

Joe DiMaggio was gone. Phil Rizzuto had seen his best baseball days. Mickey Mantle was just a first-year rookie with but half a year as a big leaguer. Yogi's bat became more important than ever. Yogi was expected to provide the big gun for the New York Yankees drive for a fourth straight pennant.

Casey Stengel had him batting fourth in the line-up, the clean-up position.

"If I can hit them half as good as Joe DiMaggio did," said Yogi, "I'll be happy."

Casey didn't have any of the doubts that beset his prize catcher. He was certain that Yogi would carry the offensive power of the team for many years to come. Still, in his usual manner, undoubtedly to bolster the confidence of his backstop, Stengel did exaggerate a bit, slapping Yogi on the back and telling him, "You'll do better than Ted Williams."

Yogi wasn't going to do as well as that Hall-of-Famer of the Boston Red Sox. But he would do well enough. What was perhaps more important was that he was the leading catcher in the American League, and the key player behind the plate. He was the man who would give aid and confidence to the Yankee pitching staff.

It may seem strange that a fellow with as little formal schooling as Yogi Berra had received could be so smart on the playing field. (There had been much written about Yogi to create the image of a comic figure on the field, to amuse his teammates; it may have been difficult for the fans to realize that Yogi was one of the most instinctive players ever to play the game.)

But Casey Stengel knew it. The men Yogi played with knew it. The men who played against him were well aware of Yogi's ability. Most important for the Yankee organization, the Yankee pitchers had confidence in Yogi. In the early formative years behind the plate, Yogi did not know the strength and weaknesses of the opposing hitters in the American League. Consequently, Manager Stengel or Coach Jim Turner would relay the appropriate sign for the pitch. Yogi never complained; after all, he was just learning his business, and he never felt that it was an insult to his intelligence.

But by 1952 Yogi was his own master, calling all the pitches without any help from his manager. It was rare now, for a pitcher to question Yogi on the type of pitch to throw to a certain hitter.

Allie Reynolds, the "Springfield Rifle," after his two no-hitters in 1951, said that Yogi had called every pitch during his great pitching efforts. If he seemed to shake off a sign every once in a while, he said, it was only to confuse the enemy.

Generally, before each game, there is a short meeting involving the manager, coaches, pitchers, and catcher, to discuss strategy and the strength and weaknesses of the opposing players. But by 1952 such meetings were conducted with Yogi the center of all activity. The pitchers would surround him and ply him with all kinds of questions. Yogi would answer those questions with short pertinent phrases that went right to the heart of the matter. He knew the strength and weakness of every hitter in the league, just as he had known all the averages, abilities, activities of the big league players, as a boy in St. Louis. It was all there in his head.

Every pitcher has his own particular temperament and has to be handled carefully and treated differently. It is not an easy task to calm a pitcher who is ruffled by an umpire, or to slow him down when his pitches are being hit, when he seems to be tiring and losing the strike zone. Yogi Berra never took a course in psychology and probably wouldn't know the scientific meaning of the word, but he had a keen knowledge of ballplayers, and a natural understanding of a pitcher's make-up. No one in the game was better at understanding his pitcher's psychological problems on the mound, and resolving them.

"You've got lots of stuff on the ball," he would say to Allie Reynolds, when he felt it necessary to walk up to the pitcher's mound. "You're going real good, Chief. Now just slow down your pitching speed. You're working too fast. Come on. Let's get this next guy, and you and me can take in that good movie we talked about."

"You've got to baby Reynolds," Yogi would later explain.

It was different with Whitey Ford.

He needled Ford, tried to get him angry, tried to get him to laugh at the same time.

"You're supposed to be a big league pitcher!" he hollered at his battery mate. "Get the ball over the plate! That's what you're paid for!"

As Yogi told it, "Ford yells right back at me, and then we're in business."

It was a different approach for different pitchers, and Yogi knew every approach and when to use it.

And Casey relied completely on the tactics and the judgment of his star backstop. If there was ever a question of whether a pitcher was losing his stuff or not, Stengel would always turn to Yogi to make the final decision. And often enough it was Yogi, noticing his pitcher weakening on the mound, would signal Casey to get someone in from the bull pen.

"This squat little man," wrote Milt Gross, one of the top New York sportswriters, in a column on Yogi, "has developed into one of the outstanding receivers of all time. He is a walking encyclopedia of the strong points of the opposing hitters and the weak points of his pitchers. He is diffident off the field but he is a strong, demanding, take-charge catcher on it. He is death on bunts and would-be base stealers."

Yogi may not have been able to understand all of the words the sportswriter wrote, but he got the drift of it well enough, and it wrinkled his face in a smile which had become familiar to both players and fans.

A picture of that plain honest face of Yogi's became a regular feature in the sports pages of the newspapers around the country, and in the sports magazines as well.

Yogi didn't repeat in the 1952 poll for Most Valuable Player, but he was the catcher again in the All-Star game. His hitting dropped slightly that season, but it was good enough to bang in 98 runs in the Yankees' drive for the pennant. His average was a fair enough .273, but he walloped 30 home runs, and that established a record for home runs hit by a catcher. Bill Dickey had established the record Yogi broke in 1937, with 29 for all the bases. No one was happier than Dickey to see Yogi Berra surpass his record. He fairly leaped out of his shoes at first base, where he was coaching for the New York club, with sheer joy and enthusiasm. After all, as far as Bill Dickey was concerned, Yogi was his protégé.

The Yankees took that World Series again in 1952, and again from a great Dodger team. This time it took New York seven games to turn the trick.

"If Berra was hitting," said the Yankee fans, "we'd take it in four straight."

But Yogi, true to past form, was far from his best in that 1952 classic.

"It was a very bad Series for me," he said.

It really wasn't all that bad. Yogi did get 6 hits in that crucial October meeting between the two champions, and two of those hits cleared the fences for four-baggers. He was to have better records, however, in the World Series yet to come.

1953 was a particularly important year for the manager of the Yankees. Casey Stengel had led the New

York club to four straight American League pennants, a record held only by two other great managers in baseball, Joe McCarthy with the same Yankee organization and John McGraw of New York Giants fame. Casey wanted to break that record, make it five straight championships for the American League New York club. Yogi Berra, as Casey expected, was going to be a great help.

"My Great Big Beautiful Doll," Old Casey called him.

"Berra is the most valuable player on the squad," Stengel said for the press so that Yogi could grin with great satisfaction reading the news item in the papers. "He can play any of six positions on the diamond," Stengel said, which must have made Yogi do a little thinking; all he had ever played for the Yankees was catcher and right fielder for any length of time that really counted.

Berra's hitting was good that season, as was generally expected. His work behind the plate continued to grow in stature.

Yogi talked a blue streak, wearing his mask and shin guards. He was a great talker. He was constantly there with some remark for the umpire on practically every pitch.

"That was a good call," he said, when the call was in favor of the Yanks.

"You missed that one," he said, when he didn't like the call. "That was a strike."

If the calls went against the Yankees with anything like persistency, Yogi would put on an elegant dramatic performance, with words to suit.

He would pull off his mask, pump the ball in his

glove, and look like a kid who had had the lollipop taken out of his mouth.

"That one came in right at the letters, right in the middle of the plate. How could you miss it?"

Sometimes Yogi was a little rougher with his speech, especially in the close games.

"You got hit in the head once too much," he yelled at umpire Cal Hubbard, who had once been a professional football player.

"You should have worn your helmet when you played ball," he snapped at another ex-pro football player turned umpire, Hank Soar.

Of course there were times when Yogi became a little too emotional about a call at home plate, kicked the dirt around, and had to be restrained by his own teammates before being finally ejected from the ball park by the umpire.

But no manager objects to such outbursts of temper on the part of their ballplayers. The will to win is a necessary ingredient in the make-up of anyone who wants to make and stay in the big leagues. And everyone knows that anyone worth the price of his uniform and salary, from the manager down, is sometimes going to be kicked out of a game, battling for what he believes is a right decision.

Of course, Yogi didn't confine his conversation to the umpire alone. He was constantly talking to the man up at bat; that is, Yogi did the talking and the batter, trying to concentrate on his job, did his best not to hear him. And no doubt much of Yogi's talking to the batter in the box was meant in the friendliest fashion possible. But Yogi was no fool. His talking to the batters had more purpose than small talk generally intends. He knew it, and the batter knew it.

"How is your cousin in Detroit?"

"It sure is a nice day for a ball game."

"Do you find that high sun bothering you in right field? Why don't you use your sun glasses?"

Sometimes a player could take that constant jabber, but it never failed to affect his concentration.

"My cousin's fine," the hitter would answer.

"Sure it's a great day for a game."

"Talk to me after the game, will you?"

More often it was, "Why don't you shut that big mouth of yours?"

Sometimes the batter even threatened to complain to the umpire.

"Why don't you tell this clown to shut up?"

At such moments, with utter aplomb, Yogi would say, "All right. I don't have to talk to you. I don't never have to talk with you. Let's call it quits."

Nobody, however, really complained to the umpire. Everybody liked Yogi. He was the friendliest of ball-players. During practice sessions, as often as not, he was over in the visiting team's dugout, or at its batting practice cage, chatting away, passing the time of day, inquiring after their health and the well-being of their families.

"We'll have to get you a visiting team uniform," quipped a Yankee one day, but nothing could get in the way of Yogi's natural interest in the people around him, or of the honest-to-goodness concern he had for them.

"Naïve," one sportswriter said of Yogi. "He's the most naïve player in baseball."

"What's this "knave" mean?" asked Yogi of his teammates, misreading the word.

"Naïve," they said, and they explained what it meant.

Yogi scratched his head.

"I suppose that's good," he said, but he wasn't sure. That uncertainty was characteristic of his naïveté.

He wasn't naïve, however, with his bat. Not in 1953. He just missed the .300 mark for his batting average, but he was good enough for 149 hits, 27 of them home runs, and he whacked home 108 more runs for the Yankees in what turned out to be a most successful season for the New York club.

The Yankees took an early lead in the race and no one came near to catching up with them. They finished the season 6½ games ahead of the second-place Cleveland Indians, and good old Casey Stengel hit the record books for managing a major league team to five straight league championships.

They beat the Dodgers, too, the Brooklyn club that had become their annual rival, for the World Championship, this time taking the World Series in six games. And this time, for once, Yogi's bat proved an important factor in the victory.

He had gone 0 for 4 in the All-Star game. This, too, was an annual feature: Yogi's selection to the All-Star team and the failure of his bat in that interleague game. It was different, however, where it really counted: in those games against the champions of the National League.

In the 1953 World Series, Yogi suddenly discovered a liking for Dodger pitching. He hammered out 9 hits in 21 times at bat, one of them a homer, for a mean

111

average of .429. He also batted home 4 valuable runs to make the Yankee win that much more decisive.

That homer, incidentally, had President Dwight D. Eisenhower talking. He had watched the ball game on TV, just before a press conference. When he came into the room, where all the newspapermen and TV correspondents were gathered and waiting for him, he didn't open his introductory remarks with some reference to some urgent foreign or domestic problem. No. He talked about the game he had just seen on his TV screen.

"I received a terrific kick out of Berra's home run," President Ike Eisenhower said, still picturing the clout. "That fellow really slammed that one out of the park."

Yogi's statistics for 1953, his play behind the plate, were, if anything, an improvement on his 1952 performance. He missed the Most Valuable Award citation, however, in 1953, coming in second to Al Rosen of the Cleveland Indians. Al had had a phenomenal season and led the league in every category of hitting. He had been magnificent in the field, too, playing first base, shortstop, and third base brilliantly. He was named first on every one of the ballots of the twenty-four sportswriters around the country.

Yogi didn't complain. He couldn't. He had been voted second in that MVP race. Besides, he was pleased with his first really good World Series performance. As to the President's remarks, remarks which were quickly repeated to the kid from the Hill, there were no words; just that big, familiar and lovable grin.

Chapter 14

It was a good year for the Yankees in 1954, but not good enough. They ended the season with 103 victories, enough wins in any normal race to guarantee the league championship. But this was no ordinary race and the Cleveland Indians, with Bobby Avila capturing the batting championship with an amazing average of .341, Larry Doby banging out 32 home runs to lead the league in that department, and Bob Lemon and Early Wynn each a 23-game winner, romped home as the American League champions with 111 wins. The New York club, after five straight pennants, had to be satisfied with second place in the final standings.

It was a year of triumph and honors for Yogi Berra. Even before the baseball teams reported to Florida for spring training, all kinds of honors came to the boy from the Hill. He had already been the recipient of any number of plaques and trophies from a variety of civic organizations and fan clubs around the country. The tributes began to multiply.

In January 1954 the New York Athletic Club voted Yogi the top professional athlete in the state of New

Jersey, where the Berra family were now established in a very comfortable home.

The New York Chapter of the B'nai B'rith, not to be outdone, named him the top professional athlete of the New York Metropolitan area, then threw a big dinner in his honor.

The Yankee organization fell right in line. They called a press conference with the express purpose of honoring their star catcher, a conference complete with a luncheon and the formal signing by Yogi of his 1954 contract which called for a salary of $43,000.

The most outstanding player of the state of New Jersey and the Metropolitan New York area responded by belting the ball in mid-season fashion at the Yankees' spring training camp. This may have been pleasant news for the New York fans; Yogi was worried by his performance.

"I never have a good season when I hit good down here in spring training," he said.

He was generally a slow starter, did nothing with his bat before the season actually got under way, and he was hitting at an amazing average of .458 in the pre-season exhibition games.

"I'm worried about it," he said. "It's all right for rookies, trying to beat the cut-off. They've got to hit to stay. But me? This could be a bad year."

As a matter of fact, it was perhaps the best year in Yogi Berra's long career. He banged out 179 hits, 28 doubles, 6 triples, and 22 home runs, for a batting average of .307. He reached his record runs-batted-in high with 125. He got more votes than anyone else in either league when the fans turned in their ballots for All-Star teams, and after some very dry seasons, he got 2 for 4 in that mid-year classic, for an average of .500.

Yogi was using a lighter bat in 1954. He had always used a 35-ounce club. This year he changed for a 33½-ounce one.

"The bat gets heavier when you get older," said Yogi, "but don't call me the old man."

Yogi was only twenty-nine years old. He still had a good number of seasons left in that bat and glove of his. Still, he believed, and maybe he was right, that using the lighter bat made his 1954 season such a magnificent one for him.

The most valuable recognition of his work for the year, however, did not come until all the baseball uniforms, gloves, bats, and caps had been put into moth balls for the while. It came with the annual baseball writers' selection of the most valuable player for the past season.

It had to be a close vote, as everyone expected. There were a lot of candidates for the honor. And no one was surprised by what might be called the photo finish.

The batting stars for the Cleveland Indians, Bobby Avila and Larry Doby, each polled five first places in the race. Minnie Minoso, the slugger for the Chicago White Sox, was named twice. But Yogi, that broad-muscled mainstay of the Yankees, received seven and came home with enough second- and third-place votes to come out on top of that most valuable heap.

Lemon polled 179 votes, Minoso 189, Avila 203, Doby 210, and Yogi 230. It was just about as close as the balloting could have been but—for the second time in his baseball career—Yogi Berra was declared the Most Valuable Player in the American League for 1954.

What was more important to Yogi was that he continued to win the confidence, the approval, even the love of not only the New York fans, but of fans everywhere in the baseball world.

"Yogi, how'd you get the Yankees to give you so much money this year?" Roy Campanella, the great Brooklyn Dodger catcher, asked Yogi Berra just before a pre-season game between the rival Dodgers and the Yankees, at the Yankees' Fort Lauderdale, Florida, training camp. A huge crowd of transplanted New York and Brooklyn rooters were on hand to cheer for their respective favorites as the 1955 season warmed up.

Yogi Berra grinned at Campy's query. "Do you believe everything you read in the papers, Roy?"

"Not exactly, but, gee, you sure got somebody's number. Somebody on the Yankee club must like you."

"Who you kidding?" Berra continued. "You're getting more money than I am."

The two catching stars, who were voted the Most Valuable Players in their respective leagues, shook their heads and grinned. They had just signed their 1955 contracts for a reported $50,000 for Berra and $48,500 for Campy.

"I hear you bought yourself a big boat too," Berra said.

"Just you call me Commodore! Just call me Commodore!" Campy, who had just bought an expensive 41-foot cabin cruiser, answered grandly.

"Go 'way," said the former Navy man Berra.

"You'll get seasick. And I hear that you also got a big new home out in Glenn Cove, Long Island, huh?"

"A ranch home—a big one and only five years old," said Campy.

"Whitey Ford lives out your way. He'll probably come over to get a free ride on your boat," chortled Yogi.

"I sure hope he does," said Campy. "He's a great guy."

The conversation continued as the two catchers watched the Yankees take their final batting practice.

"Are those some special kind of bats?" Berra pointed to two baseball bats in a corner of the bat rack.

Campy picked one of the bats up and started swinging it, unleashing his strong arms in a graceful, warm-up motion. "I swing these extra heavy bats for 10 to 15 minutes every day just to keep my swing in the groove. Say Yogi," he said, "don't your hands get sore every spring?"

"No."

"Mine do."

"Mine burn some, until I get them toughened," Berra conceded.

"During the game, I use a very small-handled bat," said Campy. "But I use a beeswax mixture in place of resin to get a better grip on the bat. Sometimes I use black-pine tar."

"I don't put anything on my bats," Berra said. "I use an R-43 type bat. Sometimes when you don't try to hit a home run, that's when you get them. I guess it's a matter of relaxing and then timing. There are times when you swing for homers and times you don't. There are times when I just want to meet the ball squarely, for that base hit."

"You're right, Yogi. Timing is everything," said Campy. "I talk to myself all the time during a game. Not out loud, though. I tell myself not to swing too hard at a certain pitch when I'm batting. I just meet the ball squarely, try to get a single to score that important one run.

"I try to plan things in my own mind before they actually happen," Campanella continued. "For instance, one of our pitchers throws his curve ball low, so I say to myself beforehand, 'I've got to be in position to block it if he throws it in the dirt.'

"When I'm catching, I warn myself, watch this fellow. I think he is anticipating a curve ball or a fast ball. A lot of batters will take a pitch if it's right down the middle. The average young boy doesn't want to be a catcher," Campy said, "because the equipment is too expensive. It'll run more than a hundred dollars, and a boy's father don't want to spend that kind of money, so many boys never get a chance to catch while they're young. A boy will buy a fielder's glove for ten dollars."

"I don't even remember where I got my first mitt," Yogi tried to recall. "My brothers all played baseball, and I used to watch them. They all had the ability to play in the big leagues, but in those days an Italian family could not afford the luxury and sacrifice necessary that would allow the boys time just to play baseball. But when I grew up, I was fortunate enough to get the support of our priest and other family members.

118

Berra looks as if he is getting heavier, but in 1963 he could still hit home runs. Here he is being congratulated by Frank Crosetti as he rounds third base after hitting a 3-run home run against the Angels. *(Wide World Photos)*

Even in the bowling alley that he ran with Phil Rizzuto, Yogi takes time to sign autographs. *(Wide World Photos)*

It isn't only the young ballplayers who chew bubble gum. Here is Sam Mele, who was manager of the Minnesota Twins in 1964, practicing bubble blowing while Berra, the manager of the Yankees, watches pregame activities. *(Associated Press Wire Photo)*

Yogi seems to have premonitions of disaster as he and first baseman Joe Pepitone watch the club work out for the opening game of the 1964 World Series. *(Associated Press Photo)*

In 1966 Yogi was a coach with the New York Mets. Here he watches Ken Boyer, left, and Jim Hickman doing calisthenics in spring training. *(Wide World Photos)*

You can't keep your temper all the time. Here Yogi and umpire Ed Sudol have a pointing contest during a 1966 game between the Mets and the Atlanta Braves. Sudol said the ball was foul, Yogi said it was fair. You can guess who won the argument. *(Wide World Photos)*

Yogi Berra, the new manager of the New York Mets, gives some advice to outfielder Rusty Staub in 1972. *(Wide World Photos)*

Managers do a lot of smiling during spring training. Here is Yogi with the Los Angeles Dodgers manager, Walter Alston, in St. Petersburg, Florida, in 1973. *(Wide World Photos)*

They pressured my dad into giving me a chance to play ball."

"When I was a small boy, I'd catch with any kind of glove," Campanella said. "We never had any shin guards or protectors, but I had a mask. I never wore it because I thought I couldn't see with all them wires and things across, but one day I got hit right in the middle of my forehead. After that I wore that mask. I was very fortunate. In twenty years in baseball I've only had one bone broken. My thumb."

Campy reached over to one of the wooden shelves and knocked on wood. "Catcher's hands are terrible," he sighed.

Suddenly, both men were aware of their hands.

Their hands were fine looking, sturdy, and uncalloused. They matched their palms against the other's, Berra's left upon Campy's right.

"They're both the same size." Berra sounded surprised. "Except your thumb is bigger," said Yogi.

"That's the one I'm always hurting."

Then Yogi looked at the middle finger of his right hand. It was thicker than the rest. "I've split this one three times."

"I've had a bad knee and a bad hand," Campanella said.

"I've had a busted wrist and a broken wrist," Berra said without explaining the difference.

Yogi looked at his left index finger and wiggled it. "Keeping it outside the glove protects me from getting a bone bruise . . . All them knuckle balls. That's what hurts. But speaking of catchers being different," he said, "I don't think you're going to see every

119

catcher throw the same way either—Campy, you don't take a step when you throw the ball."

"I'm not flat-footed when I throw," Campy said. "I'm always on balance. You have to be. When I'm lining myself up to receive the ball, that's when I take my step. When I get the ball, all I have to do is stride and throw. I don't have to take any more steps."

"Your feet are very important," Berra said. "When I turned professional they said I had a pretty good arm but no control of it. Bill Dickey helped me correct that. He told me to move my feet, and I did and I started getting accuracy. When I throw, I take my step. It helps me get distance with my throw. . . . That was the main thing wrong with me. Dickey said I had ability to be a catcher.

"I was bad on the balls thrown in the dirt," Yogi continued, "and Dickey taught me how to block a ball. You have to get in front of the ball, that is the main thing. You got to be ready at all times to block the ball. Don't let it get by you."

"A lot of catchers blink," said Campanella, "but if you blink when the batter swings at the pitch, you're losing the flight of the ball momentarily, and then you have to locate it again and you lose valuable time."

"And the guy may foul the ball. If you blink you lose sight of the ball," Berra said.

"Like the time when Allie Reynolds was pitching a no-hit game," Campanella recalled. "I was watching it on television, and Ted Williams hit a real high foul, and Yogi you jumped at the ball and missed it. I kidded you about it later."

"I was lucky that time," Yogi came back. "Lucky because Reynolds got Williams to pop up again."

"Yogi, it's just about time for this ball game. I don't want to wish you too much good luck. Those Yankees and you have had enough. But I will say, that I don't want you to get hurt," said Campanella.

"Roy, thanks a lot. I sure wish you luck . . . lots of good luck. But not today."

They shook hands warmly, and both men returned to their respective dugouts for the start of the game.

In 1955 the Yankees came back to win the American League flag for Casey Stengel and to start yet another string of consecutive American League championships. And, once again, it was Yogi Berra who provided the spark with his fine play behind the plate and his tremendous hitting.

Yogi drove out 27 home runs in that pennant drive, among them was his 200th homer, putting him in a class with Bill Dickey and Chicago's great Gabby Hartnett, the only two other catchers who at that time had hit 200 or more homers in their baseball careers.

In the National League, the Brooklyn Dodgers with such super-Dodger heroes as Jackie Robinson, Gil Hodges, Duke Snider, Pee Wee Reese, Roy Campanella, and Carl Furillo swept aside all opposition to win the coveted flag and then in seven breathtakingly exciting games swept by the Yankees for their first World Series win since 1916.

The Yankees beat the Dodgers in the first two games, which were played in Yankee Stadium, but the Brooks battled back gamely, to capture the next three to lead the series. The Yankees won the sixth game.

The seventh and deciding game at Yankee stadium

pitted the Dodgers fine hurler, Johnny Podres, and the great Yankee left-hander, Tommy Byrne, and both pitchers were in marvelous form. The Dodgers jumped off to a 2–0 lead and it looked like the end of the road for the Bronx Bombers.

Then, suddenly, for just a moment, Podres weakened and walked Billy Martin. Gil McDougald beat out an infield hit for a clean single, and there were two men on when Yogi Berra stepped in to hit.

Yogi had been the standout hitter for the Yankees up to this point; had slugged out 10 hits in 24 trips to the plate for a .417 average. It was Yogi's finest Series performance since joining the Yankees, and the huge crowd reacted with a tremendous roar as he approached the plate.

The roar of the crowd turned into a volcano of sound as Yogi lashed at the first pitch thrown by Podres and slammed the ball toward the left-field foul line. It was a tremendous drive, high and wide, and the ball curved sharply toward the lower rung of the seats.

Out in left field, Sandy Amoros took off with the crack of the bat, and headed for the towering Berra drive. He tore recklessly after the ball and somehow, just as the ball started to drop into the lower boxes, Sandy was there. He stuck his glove into the stands, caught the ball and tumbled into the boxes.

It was one of the great World Series plays, and certainly pulled the game out for the Dodgers, as they went on to win the game and the World Series, 4–3.

The December vote for the Most Valuable Player Award was another close one. Ted Williams got one first place on the ballot; Al Kaline, the Detroit slugger, got four. The Indians' Al Smith and Yogi were tied with seven each. It was the second and third positions in the balloting that made the difference between winning and losing the top honors, and again, as Casey Stengel had predicted in spring, it was Yogi Berra who was named the Most Valuable Player in the American League.

Only four other men have been named Most Valuable Player three times, and they are all Hall-of-Famers. There was the irrepressible Jimmy Foxx, the incomparable Joe DiMaggio, that Man, Stanley Musial, and after Yogi Berra had reached that pinnacle, the great and gallant Roy Campanella.

Yogi became thirty years old in 1955. At thirty, a ballplayer knows that there aren't too many years left in his career. Yogi was not going to win any more of those Most Valuable Player awards, but in 1955 it was obvious to all, ballplayers and fans alike, that Yogi was a vital cog in the Yankee organization, and would remain so for a long, long time to come.

Still, like most smart professional athletes, Yogi knew that there was a limit to a man's years in the sports arena, whatever that sport may be. A man's legs begin to give out and he can't run the way he did in his youth. His eyes begin to lose some of their sharpness. His reactions begin to slow down. It doesn't happen all at once, except in rare cases, but it does happen, no matter how well a man keeps in shape, no matter how careful a player looks out for himself, time finally slows all of us down to a walk.

Maybe Yogi didn't look ahead to the days when he could no longer be a whirlwind on the bunted ball, throw the ball like a bullet to second base, slam over the fences and into the bleacher seats, but there were others around him who did.

"You need a business manager to help you plan for the future," said his friend, Ugo Antonucci.

"What do I know about business?" came back Yogi.

"I'm willing. I'd be glad to be your business manager," said Antonucci, and strangely enough perhaps, it was Yogi's interests and only Yogi's interests that concerned his friend.

"I don't like stocks," said Yogi. "I don't trust them. I don't like anything about putting your money into anything but a bank. I'm a ballplayer."

"Sure, you're a ballplayer," said Antonucci. "For how long? And what do you do about money when you're not a ballplayer?"

It did take some talking, but Yogi finally acquiesced, with a bit of prodding by his old pal Phil Rizzuto. Under the guidance of their old friend, Ugo Antonucci, Phil Rizzuto and Yogi organized a partnership to build a bowling alley in Clifton, New Jersey. The partnership proved successful. The bowling alley, which was opened in 1958 with forty alleys, a snack bar, a cocktail lounge and restaurant, was equally successful, perhaps to Yogi's surprise.

He feels pretty good about that investment and that bowling alley now.

"If we don't run into a depression," he says, remembering the depression years of his youth, "that bowling alley takes care of Phil's family and my family for the rest of our lives."

There were other investments Yogi would make, the most famous of them the money he put into the Yoo-

124

Hoo Chocolate Drink Company. He is the vice president of that company and enjoys promoting its product.

"It's a good drink," he says. "I like it myself."

How could anyone say "No" to an endorsement like that?

Chapter 15

There was considerable talk in the spring training camps about Yogi Berra's chances for breaking still another all-time baseball record in 1956. No player in the history of the game had ever won three consecutive Most Valuable Player awards, but the way Yogi was blasting the ball, there were any number of sportswriters, as well as active ballplayers, who believed he could repeat his 1954 and 1955 performances.

Not Yogi. At least, he had his doubts.

"Too much competition," he said.

He mentioned Al Rosen of Cleveland, Whitey Ford, Detroit's Al Kaline, and others.

"And if you ask me," he continued, "it'll be Mickey Mantle, if he doesn't get hurt. Mickey was hurt most of those first couple of years, but right now, he could go on to be one of the greatest stars in the history of baseball."

Mickey Mantle had been a great all-around athlete for his Commerce, Oklahoma, high school teams. He played baseball, basketball, and football, and in his senior year, Mickey was the leading halfback for the

Commerce eleven. His fine running, passing, and kicking led Commerce to one of their best seasons, and Mickey was offered scholarships to some twenty-five colleges.

But Mickey loved baseball, and his tremendous hitting with Commerce and several local sand-lot teams won him a contract and a bonus of $1,000 with the New York Yankees. The Yankees shipped the seventeen-year-old Mantle to their Independence team of the Kansas, Oklahoma, Missouri League, and Mickey responded by tearing up the league. He slugged home runs and was the batting star of the league with a .313 average. The following year Mickey was promoted to the class C Joplin club and responded by driving out 27 homers and hitting the ball for a remarkable .383 average.

Mantle was invited to the Yankee spring training camp at Phoenix, Arizona, in 1951 and promptly began to slug the ball to every corner of the park. His tremendously long drives, his great speed in going down to first base, aroused the attention of all the sportswriters. Casey Stengel had invited Mickey to camp with the intention of sending him back to the minors for further seasoning, but Mickey's amazing spring showing changed all that, and Casey inserted him into the regular line-up.

Careful handling by Stengel, who hovered over Mickey like a son, brought results, and within a five-year-period Mantle developed into one of the all-time Yankee stars.

Yogi, Whitey Ford, and Billy Martin took young Mickey Mantle under their wing, and the three Yankee stars and the young Commerce slugger became inseparable, on and off the field—and their escapades had Stengel in a constant frenzy of worry.

By 1956 Mickey Mantle had put all his skills together, and when it came time for the rating for the Most Valuable Player, Mickey Mantle, the brightest new Yankee star, won all the honors. He led the league in batting with a .353 average, hit 52 home runs, and brought in 130 runs, and just as Yogi had predicted earlier, Mantle won every first-place ballot cast by the sportswriters for a perfect score of 396 points and the coveted MVP award.

The year 1956 was not a bad one for Yogi either. In the first 33 games of the season he drove out 12 home runs and was hitting the ball at a .353 average, until a pulled muscle benched him. Nonetheless, Yogi polled more votes than any other player in the league, with the exception of his teammate Mickey Mantle, in the voting for the All-Star line-ups. By mid-September, he had hammered out the 237th homer of his career, breaking the previous record for home runs hit by catcher, Gabby Hartnett's record of 236. He missed a .300 batting average for the season by just 2 points, walloped 30 homers, and drove 105 Yankees over the plate. It was good enough a record to make him a candidate for the MVP award, as the sportswriters, players, and fans had expected. They just hadn't reckoned on Mantle, as Yogi has seen it in early April of the year.

There was one serious concern Yogi had, in 1956, and it had nothing to do with baseball.

Back in St. Louis, his mother was suffering severely with diabetes. Yogi was well aware of the serious situation and one wonders what he would have done with his bat if his mind hadn't been back in Missouri so much of the time.

The regular season play, with the Yankees breezing to another pennant, had just about ended when Yogi got word that his mother was to have a leg amputated because of her diabetes.

"It's the only way we can save her life," said the doctors in St. Louis.

The operation, fortunately, proved successful, and undoubtedly affected Yogi's performance in the World Series, which was to make baseball history.

Yogi got 2 hits in his 2 times at bat in the 1956 All-Star game, for an average of 1.000, which established a personal record for the Yankee slugger. He enjoyed one of the best World Series, once again, as the Yankees tangled with their bitter rivals, playing one more time against the National League Dodgers. Yogi's average at the plate was well up there with .360. And he belted 3 of the 9 hits he garnered out of the park, for home runs. One of those homers, against the Brooklyn ace, Don Newcombe, was a grand-slammer, scoring 4 runs for the New York club. It was the first and only grand-slam home run Yogi was to hit in all his World Series play.

In the final game of the classic, Yogi hit 2 for all the bases.

"That one was for my mom," he said, coming into the dugout after the first of his two mighty clouts that afternoon.

Yogi's mind was still with his mother.

"I wish she could have been here to see it."

There were more dramatic items for Yogi in that Series. When the final out was made in the last of the

129

seven games of the classic, which the Yankees won again, and all the statistics were in, there was one more record to be put into the books for the kid from the Hill.

Back in 1928 the Iron-Man, Lou Gehrig, had established a record for the Series, batting in 9 runs for the Yankees. Yogi Berra, in 1956, broke that record. There were 10 runs he hammered in for the New York club, setting a mark that would stand for years to come.

The most dramatic moment of that famous series, however, did not belong to Yogi alone. It belonged to everyone who was in the baseball park that afternoon, to the millions who watched it on television, listened to it on radio, to the whole sports world. And the central figure of that dramatic moment was Don Larsen.

Don Larsen had something of a reputation as a playboy, a fellow who didn't go in much for following the rules too seriously. That afternoon, October 8, 1956, there was nothing of the playboy about the big, six-foot-four, 220-pound right-hand pitcher. He was all business, and serious business, too.

His opponent that afternoon was the "Barber," Sal Maglie, a crafty curve-ball pitcher. For the first three and a third innings, both Maglie and Larsen pitched perfect games, not a man reaching base on a hit or a walk. With two out in the fourth inning, Mickey Mantle got hold of a fast one and sent it screaming over the barriers for a home run. That run was going to be important, though the Yankees added another run to it in a later inning.

Meanwhile, big Don Larsen continued to pour them

in, his pitches always on their target, holding the Dodgers to no hits, no walks.

Gil McDougald grabbed a ball that had caromed off the glove of Andy Carey, playing third base, and whipped it to first, nipping the speedster Jackie Robinson by no more than an eyelash. That was in the second inning. Duke Snider missed a home run by inches with a smash into the right-field stands, and Sandy Amoros duplicated the smash in the fifth inning. But both balls were caught. Mickey Mantle made a great running catch of a liner Gil Hodges sent deep into left center field. But not a Dodger reached first base, not on a hit, not on a walk.

Yogi, crouched behind home plate, tried to be as nonchalant as possible. He had a sense of history in the making as he concentrated on each batter; calmly talked to his pitcher, and signaled the field positions, as each Dodger came to bat.

Gil McDougald made a great stop and a lightning throw to first to beat the super-fast Junior Gilliam to the bag. This was in the seventh inning, and Don Larsen, with his no-wind-up pitch had not allowed a single Dodger hit, and had not walked anyone.

The 64,159 fans in Yankee Stadium were now yelling with each pitch. The tension had begun to reach its breaking point.

In the dugout, after the seventh inning, the Yankees were as silent as a congregation listening to the minister deliver his Sunday sermon. Larsen sat quietly on the bench. He knew the situation. He knew that six more outs and he might accomplish a feat never achieved in World Series history. Yogi, who was never known to

131

have stopped talking for more than a minute during a game, was silent.

In the eighth inning, Gil Hodges sent a wicked low line drive at Andy Carey. Carey stabbed for it just inches off the ground. The ball bounced up. He picked it off while it was still in the air. Hodges was out, but Carey whipped the ball to first, to make sure. That was as close as the Dodgers came to getting a man on base in that eighth.

It was now the ninth inning. Don Larsen was just three away from a perfect game, the kind of game every pitcher, young or old, dreams of; three outs from perhaps the most dramatic performance in baseball, the first no-hit, no-run, game in the story of the fall classic.

Carl Furillo, always a dangerous hitter, was the first man up for the Dodgers in that nerve-tingling ninth inning, the twenty-fifth Dodger to face Don Larsen.

Berra was calling for the ball over the plate. A little low, a little wide, a bit inside, fast ball, let-up, curve, it had to be in the strike zone.

"Nobody is going to walk to spoil this one," he said to himself.

Furillo fouled one off. He fouled off another. He fouled pitches three and four, and finally fouled out to Hank Bauer. It was an easy play. One man was out. Two more for the perfect game.

The players tensed in the field. In the stands, the 64,159 fans had sent up a din that wouldn't let up.

Roy Campanella stepped up to the plate. There weren't many better clutch hitters in the game.

Berra crouched behind the plate, wig-wagged his signals with his stubby fingers. Larsen nodded his head, toed the pitcher's rubber, let go with a fast one from his no-wind-up position.

Campanella, always a threat to break up the game with a long one, belted the ball way out into left field. It landed in the upper deck in left field, but it was foul.

Don Larsen took a deep breath.

So did Yogi.

Again the pitch, and this time Roy could do no better than roll it down to Billy Martin for another easy play and the second out of the inning.

One more to go.

There was bedlam in the stands.

On the field, the Yankees moved restlessly around their positions.

Walter Alston, managing the Dodgers, called Sal Maglie back to the dugout, sent Dale Mitchell, a veteran left-hander, to pinch-hit for him.

Dale Mitchell swung two heavy practice bats. He'd drop one on the way to the plate. The other bat was intended to whip that ball through the diamond, to break up the perfect game Don Larsen all but had in the record books.

"Nothing gets through here," said Billy Martin to Joe Collins, the Yankee first baseman, nervously.

"If it comes this way," said Collins, not a whit more nervously, "I'll throw myself at it. I don't care if it's an error. I don't want to see a base hit."

Gil McDougald was talking to no one in particular.

"One more. Don't lose him. One more."

Andy Carey tried to reason with himself.

"Play it like any other ball that comes your way. It's the last out. Let's get it and win the ball game!"

Yogi studied slugging Dale Mitchell at the plate. He was the last man, the man who was the last barrier to the record-making perfect game.

Dale Mitchell swung his bat in that menacing manner common to so many other ballplayers.

Yogi, crouched, called for the fast ball.

It cut across the plate, but it was low.

"Ball one!"

Yogi called for a slider.

It caught the corner of the plate for a strike, and the din in the stands grew louder.

Another fast ball, and this time Mitchell took a cut at it and missed.

"Strike two!"

Nobody could hear anybody for the noise that came from the Yankee fans, all up on their feet in the Stadium.

Berra called for another fast one.

Mitchell fouled it off.

"Don't everybody manage," hollered a nervous Casey Stengel in the dugout, as if he could read all the thoughts of all his players on the field. "Let him alone."

He might as well have been speaking to himself. Nothing could be heard in Yankee Stadium for the roar that came out of the stands and seemed to swallow the air.

Casey was on the steps of the dugout now. He motioned Hank Bauer and Mickey Mantle to move to the right.

Bauer took four steps to the right, Mickey three.

Yogi was in his crouch. He gave Don Larsen the sign. Larsen shook it off.

Yogi changed the sign. Larsen shook him off again.

This little bit of play acting had been performed before in the game. It was meant to confuse the hitter.

Yogi came back to his original signal. Don Larsen nodded his head. They felt sure now that they had Mitchell guessing.

Yogi called for the fast ball.

The fast ball swept across the heart of the plate.

Mitchell, evidently confused by the wig-wagging that he had witnessed, started to swing at the ball, then pulled back. It was all over!

"Strike three!" snapped Babe Pinelli, umpiring behind the plate, and Yogi was leaping into the arms of his pitcher, and the crowd went wild.

They had a right to go wild. They had been witness to the first perfect game ever pitched in World Series competition. It was a day and a game that ballplayers, fans, the whole baseball world will never forget.

"When it looked like he'd make it," the sportswriters asked Yogi, "in the seventh and eighth and ninth innings, what did you say to Larsen?"

"What can you say to a fellow when he's pitching like Don was pitching? What can you say, when his fast ball has all that stuff on it? Nothing!"

This was typical of Yogi, giving a man all the credit he was due, letting a man bask in the sun of his glorious performance. Not a word about his own contribution to that great game, not a word about the mastery with which he handled his pitcher, guided him, encouraged him, through a feat that had never been witnessed before. That's the way Yogi was, and still is: the straightforward, simple, honest man he will always be.

But Don Larsen, even while the Yankee clubhouse was celebrating the great pitcher's fantastic achievement on the diamond, and wildly, wouldn't allow Yogi to bury himself in his modesty.

"Yogi called every pitch. Sure I shook off a couple of signs, but that was to get them guessing, and it worked, didn't it?"

"You did it! You did it!" they were shouting all around the clubhouse, getting out of their sweated uniforms, hopping into the showers.

"I did it," said Don Larsen. "But let me tell you I was nervous, and I was scared, too. Especially in those last three innings."

"You did it, Don!"

"My knees were knocking and I was trembling all over. Let me tell you, I'm glad I had Yogi back there. He did all my thinking for me. I took all his signs. Give him credit for it. He's the greatest catcher in the game!"

The record books read that Don Larsen pitched the first perfect game in World Series play. Don Larsen, and a whole lot of other baseball people, would like those record books to report that it was Yogi Berra, "the greatest catcher in the game," who quarterbacked that brilliant history-making performance.

Chapter 16

Yogi Berra headed straight for St. Louis, once the New York Yankees had wrapped up that glorious World Series of 1956. He was anxious about the well-being of his mother. The operation she had undergone had been successful, according to the surgeons. Nevertheless, Yogi had to see for himself. No one could have been more attached to his mother or loved her more.

While he was in his home town, pleased with the way his mother was getting along, and feeling much easier about it, he attended a luncheon of the Professional and Business Men's Club of the Hill section of St. Louis to celebrate the homecoming of the local baseball hero. He didn't mind hearing, either, one of the speakers at that affair, undoubtedly in the spirit of the celebration, call Yogi the third of the great Italians. The other two were Columbus and Marconi.

Certainly it was a bit of an exaggerated tribute, being classed with the great explorer and the great inventor, but Yogi accepted it in the mood of the occasion. He responded with a little talk on the World

137

Series and the "crystal ball" he was sure Casey Stengel took to bed with him every night. In his usual manner he played down his own part in the Yankee victory, but by this time no one had to be told how important the brilliant, slugging catcher was to the New York organization.

At least, George Weiss who handled the contract deals for the New York club, didn't have to be told. Yogi hadn't returned to New Jersey with his family before he got a call from the Yankee front office.

"I'm sending you a contract for $55,000," said George Weiss.

He had long given up the business of trying to get Yogi "cheap."

"Good enough for me," said Yogi, and the deal was closed.

Yogi had traveled a long way from the days when he had to bargain, to hold out, for the kind of salary he thought he had earned.

By 1956 The Berra family had increased considerably as Carmen gave birth to her third son, Dale, born December 14, 1956. Lawrence Allen Berra, their first son, had been born in St. Louis in 1949, where Yogi and Carmen had lived with his parents on Elizabeth Street between the baseball seasons. Two years later, their second son, Timothy, had been born.

"What are your children going to look like?" Carmen had been asked by her friends before she married Yogi. "Suppose they look like him!"

Carmen hadn't been worried by the prospect. Enos Slaughter, the Cardinal slugger, had once cracked, and rather unkindly, at Yogi, "You're the only catcher I know whose face looks better with his mask on it."

138

Whether Carmen heard that ugly gibe or not, it didn't matter to her.

"He's a good man," she said, "a kind man. And I love him."

That love must have had something to do with it. All the sons in the Berra family—Dale, Lawrence, Timothy—are rugged fellows, healthy, athletic, and positively handsome.

Yogi has a beautiful family, and they live in a beautiful house. Carmen would not be satisfied until she found exactly what she was looking for, and eventually she was to find it in a new, Tudorlike mansion in Montclair.

It was a sumptuous dwelling place, and Yogi was quite taken with it.

"What a house!" he exclaimed, according to Jackie Farrell, the director of the speaking bureau for the New York Yankees public relations department. "It's got nothing but rooms!"

Jackie Farrell, along with Joe Garagiola, Yogi's constant companion of the Hill days, have told more stories about Berra than one can count. How many of them are true, how many of them are exaggerated, how many made up of whole cloth, it is difficult to say. Whatever the story, however, there is love for the man behind it.

Garagiola, on his first trip to visit Yogi in Montclair got lost. He called him on the phone.

"Yog! I'm lost!"

"Where are you?" asked Yogi.

"Somebody says I'm at the Library."

"Good. You're just a couple of blocks away. But don't go that way. Come this way."

Or:

"Nobody goes to that restaurant any more," said Yogi, according to Farrell. "It's too crowded."

And another:

"What do you think of Little League baseball?" he was asked.

"I think it's wonderful," said Yogi. "It keeps the kids out of the house."

And still another:

A little old lady, during a particularly hot day at the spring training camp, to Yogi: "Good afternoon, Mr. Berra. You look mighty cool today."

Yogi, responding, "Thank you, ma'am. You don't look too hot yourself."

There are countless more like them.

Yogi, the good-natured, lovable character, takes it all in stride.

"I guess there must be two Yogi Berras. There's the ballplayer with a beautiful wife and three great sons. Then there's the guy who reads comic books and says all those funny things.

"I know the ballplayer with the beautiful family. That's me. The other fellow ought to be writing stuff for Bob Hope and Jackie Gleason. I don't know him at all."

Don Larsen, after his perfect game in the 1956 World Series, said for the whole baseball world to hear that Yogi Berra had done all his thinking for him, behind the plate.

There weren't many in or around baseball who credited Yogi, especially in his early years, with the ability to do any thinking of any kind. They had learned, and they would continue to learn, that Berra had one of the keenest baseball minds in baseball.

Maybe some sportswriters thought Casey Stengel was pulling their legs when he called Yogi, "My assistant manager," when they were both still with the Yankees.

He wasn't kidding.

Joe Garagiola has told this story about his pal Yogi a thousand times:

Yogi had banged out three hits in a game, but in the newspapers the next day he was listed as having hit two for his four times at bat.

"How come they put down two hits?" asked the annoyed Yogi Berra. "I got three!"

He was speaking to the official scorer of the game, and complaining with considerable vehemence. Hits were very important to Yogi. The more hits, the higher the salary one could ask, and get, from the front office.

"Sorry, Yogi," apologized the official scorer. "It's a typographical error."

"What do you mean?" boiled Yogi. "Two of them was clean hits to left. The other one, the shortstop makes a perfect throw to first base, only I beat the throw."

Yogi has heard the story himself a few times. His pal Joey has told the story at more than a few banquets, where both of the boys from the Hill were honored.

"It's a funny story," says Yogi. "What difference if it's true or not? It's funny and I don't mind Joey making those imitations of me. We've been buddies a long, long time."

141

The simple facts about Yogi and all those humorous tales are that there is a grain of truth in all of them. Yogi was honest and he wasn't given to mincing words. The difficulty was that Yogi wasn't very good with words, certainly not as good as his pal, the fine ballplayer turned great sportscaster, Joe Garagiola. And, at rock bottom, there is no one more serious about things around him, particularly his family, more serious about the professional game of baseball than is the man Yogi Berra knows: Yogi Berra.

Berra gets thrown out of a game in 1973. He had argued too long with umpire Tom Gorman in a game with the Pittsburgh Pirates. *(Wide World Photos)*

Old home week. Casey Stengel, who had been Yogi's manager with the Yankees, and later managed the Mets, having a chat with the Met manager before the second World Series game of 1973 against the Oakland A's. *(Wide World Photos)*

It was all smiles on October 18, 1973. Pitchers Tug McGraw, left, and Jerry Koosman had combined for a 2–1 win over the Athletics. The Mets then led the World Series 3 games to 2, but later the roof caved in. *(Wide World Photos)*

Tim Berra has certainly grown up. Here Yogi and Mrs. Berra are seen at a game between the University of Massachusetts and the University of Vermont in 1973. Tim was a star receiver with the University of Massachusetts, and Yogi was honored that day for his role as manager of the National League pennant winners and his loyalty as a football fan. *(Wide World Photos)*

In 1974 the two managerial rivals of the 1973 World Series met again. This time Dick Williams of the Oakland A's and Yogi were managing the two All-Star teams at Pittsburgh's Three Rivers Stadium. *(Wide World Photos)*

Old friends get together. Joe Garagiola gets Yogi ready for an appearance on Joe's television show in 1975. *(Wide World Photos)*

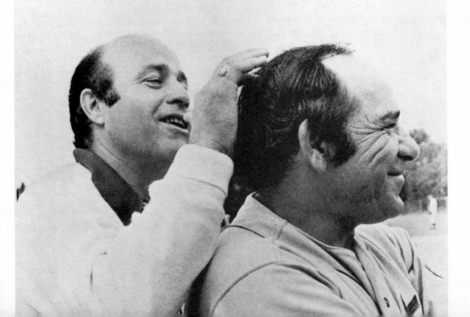

One of Yogi's last arguments as manager of the Mets. Once again it was in a game with the Pittsburgh Pirates—this time in 1975. *(Wide World Photos)*

What will the future hold for Yogi Berra, the Hall of Famer? *(Wide World Photos)*

Chapter 17

Yogi Berra reached his thirty-second birthday as the 1957 season started, and for the first time it become obvious that the Yankee backstop was really just as mortal as any other ballplayer on the diamond. He was no device created by the devil or any other kind of supernatural power for the sole purpose of menacing and destroying American League pitching. He was an athlete, and like all athletes must suffer the inevitable effects of time.

A ballplayer's arms become a little heavier with time. Even the strongest of them, like Willie Stargell who swings the bat as if he were holding nothing more than a toothpick in his hands, has had to turn to a lighter bat with the years. His eyes have begun to lose some of their sharpness. His wrist is just a little slower, snapping at the pitch. The muscles in his legs are a little less flexible. He loses a step, racing to first. His timing falls off.

It happens to all of them. There may have been

something of the unexpected, something of a surprise, when it happened to Berra. But it had to, and it did.

Nineteen fifty-seven was not one of Berra's better seasons in baseball. He opened the year well enough, smashing a single and a homer against the Washington Senators in the first game of the Yankee schedule, but except for an exceptionally bright day, that was it.

His batting fell off badly. At mid-season, he was hitting in the low .200s. He tried wearing glasses. That didn't help. He took them off. That didn't help either. He wound up the season with the lowest batting average he would ever post as a full-time Yankee regular, a poor .251, although he did bang out 24 home runs in the Yankees drive for still another pennant, the third in a row and the ninth since Yogi had donned the New York American League uniform.

Injuries, however, did slow up Yogi throughout the season.

This was the year when Larry Raines of the Cleveland Indians accidentally sent a foul tip smashing into Yogi's mask, snapping the center bar at both ends, the bar cutting deeply into Yogi's nose. Fortunately for Yogi, his eyes were untouched. The damage was limited to a broken nose. It was this freak accident that had the doctors so worried about Yogi's vision that they suggested eyeglasses. It was not his eyes, as things turned out, that bothered Yogi, but even after the broken nose was patched up, he experienced great difficulty sleeping and some difficulty breathing. This worried Yogi and affected his play behind the plate.

It was another foul tip, this time off the bat of the Dodgers' Don Zimmer, in the annual New York

Mayor's charity exhibition game, that bruised Yogi's ankle badly.

Still another foul tip, late in the season, tore into Yogi's right thumb.

Was Yogi slowing up behind the plate? Were his reflexes losing a beat? Were those foul-tip injuries avoidable? Would he have suffered them in one of his younger seasons?

Nineteen fifty-seven was also the year in which the Yankees were beaten in the World Series by the Milwaukee Braves and Lew Burdette. Lew Burdette, the pitcher who was repeatedly charged with putting some "foreign substance" on the ball, beat the New York club three times in that series and clinched the World Championship for the upstart Braves.

But Yogi, himself, didn't do badly in that fall classic. As a matter of fact, as his physical condition improved, Yogi began to pound the ball for the Yankees and he continued to slug the ball in the World Series, getting 8 hits and 1 a homer in 25 times at bat, for an average of .320. Maybe it was the late showing that saved him from a salary cut in his 1958 contract.

"He's got a few good years left in him," said Bill Dickey.

That didn't make Yogi feel much better.

"If I don't do better in fifty-eight," said the Yankee catcher, "there'll be a cut in my pay, and I won't be able to say anything about it."

Yogi did do better in 1958, but not by much. Casey began to substitute for Yogi. He would send in the rising star, Elston Howard, behind the plate, and would place Berra in the outfield.

"Crouching behind the batter can take a lot out of a fellow if he does it day in and day out."

Casey, as always, or so it seemed, made the correct decision. He valued Yogi's bat too much to leave it out of the line-up, and while the mighty Berra bat fell off in its home-run total for the season, it was good enough for 22 home runs, 115 hits and 90 runs batted in. It was good enough, too, to help the Yankees win still another American League championship and to avenge its 1957 defeat at the hands of the Braves.

The Yankees had to come from behind in that classic to win yet another of its World Championships, to do what only one other club in the history of the classic had been able to accomplish. Like the Pittsburgh Pirates against the Washington Senators in the 1925 World Series, the New Yorkers found themselves down one game to three, needing three straight victories to claim the World Championship, an almost impossible feat to perform against a league champion. But Pittsburgh did it in 1925, and the Yankees did it in 1957.

It was Yogi who, with the score of the seventh and final game tied 2–2, opened the inning with a smash to center field, good for two bases. Ellie Howard singled him home for the tie breaking run. Moose Skowron, another of the all-time Yankee sluggers, followed with a home run, scoring two more runs in that seventh inning, and the New York club had enough to win the game, put the Braves in their place, and take the championship.

"Next to DiMaggio," said Casey Stengel, as the gear for that 1958 season was put away, "in all the ten years I've been with the Yankees, that Yogi Berra is the best ballplayer I've ever managed."

There was no man in baseball that Yogi respected more than Casey. That kudo, coming from Stengel, was a comment Yogi would treasure. Among the great men Casey Stengel had managed for the New York club, in addition to Joe DiMaggio, there were Mickey Mantle, Gil McDougald, Billy Martin, Moose Skowron, "Old Reliable" Tommy Henrich, Phil Rizzuto, Hank Bauer, as well as some of the greatest hurlers the game has ever known, Vic Raschi and Whitey Ford, just to name two. To be named number two in a Stengel list of all-stars, and second only to Joe DiMaggio, a legend in his own time—was something any ballplayer would be proud to put into his scrapbook of baseball memories.

Yogi took a pay cut in his 1959 contract, as he expected he would. Still, 1959 might be considered one of the more exciting years in his career, despite the personal tragedy he suffered almost as soon as the season began.

Paulina Berra, Yogi's mother, was hospitalized early in May. This time, it was not expected that she would leave the hospital.

Yogi asked Stengel for leave to visit her in St. Louis, and of course "Old Case" wasn't going to stop a fellow from seeing his mother before she died.

There was a reservation for Yogi to fly from Kansas City, where the Yanks were playing, at noon.

He didn't take it.

At six in the morning, there was a call from the doctors in St. Louis.

"She is sinking fast. If you want to see her before she goes, you'd better get here in a hurry."

Yogi made the 7:00 A.M. plane, but when he finally got to the hospital his mother was already in the coma from which she never recovered.

Yogi leaned over her bed.

"Mom, it's Lawdie," he said, softly.

"It's me, Mom. It's Lawdie."

Yogi thinks that she heard him. She didn't speak, he says, but she moved a little.

"Mom, it's me. Lawdie," he repeated, but she would not move again.

The priest arrived and gave her Extreme Unction. She was only sixty-four years old when she died, that afternoon, with her family at her bedside.

Yogi took the rosary that she had held in her hands all the while she was going.

"I loved her very much," says Yogi.

He carries his mother's rosary with him, wherever he goes, wherever he stays.

Any day after that day in St. Louis, watching his mother go, had to be a happier day. But Yogi had some days in 1959 that must have made him especially happy.

For the second time in his baseball life, the Catholic Youth Organization voted him the most popular of all the Yankees. Five thousand CYO boys were guests at the Stadium for the presentation of the trophy.

In August, in his ninth straight appearance in the All-Star mid-season rivalry, he slammed one of Dodger Don Drysdale's fast ones for a two-run home run to win the game for the American Leaguers. He was also named the "Player of the Game."

148

Then there was the "Berra Day" dedicated by the fans and the Yankees to the slugger. It was September 19. His father and sister came in from St. Louis for it. Of course, Carmen and their three boys were there. "Days" are not given to just anybody. There had been only five other ballplayers so signally saluted by the Yankee club.

The owners of the New York franchise gave Yogi a new station wagon. Yogi's teammates gave him a silver tray with all their signatures on it. The baseball writers had their names etched on a silver plate to present to the man of the day. Joe DiMaggio, that incomparable gentleman, made a personal gift of a watch to Yogi.

In all, there were fifty-eight gifts for the slugger, among them fifty pounds of sirloin steak, a year's supply of coffee, a year's supply of pizzas (for which Yogi never lost his appetite), a hunting rifle, a fishing rod, patio furniture, and a swimming pool for his house in Montclair. There was, in addition, the sum of $9,800, collected and amassed by fans and businessmen, and a truckload of baseball equipment.

Yogi gave that $9,800 to New York's Columbia University for a fund to be known as the Berra Scholarship fund. It pays $500 a year toward the tuition of a boy whose athletic and scholastic abilities merit it, and whose need warrants it.

It pleases Yogi to know that though he himself had a tough time making it through eight grades of public school, he can now help a youngster make his way through college, and Columbia University at that!

The truckload of baseball equipment, bats, balls, gloves, etc., went to Italy, to the Italian Boys' Town,

149

and Yogi and Carmen, thanks to the two round-trip tickets they received from Alitalia Airlines, delivered them in person to the grateful youngsters.

While in Italy, Carmen and Yogi did a little sight-seeing. They went to the museums and the shrines, took in the great paintings in the great churches. In Milan, they went to the opera, the famous La Scala.

"How did you like it?" they asked Yogi.

"Pretty good," he said. "Even the music was nice."

In Rome, they had an audience with the Pope.

"I understand you had an audience with the Pope," said Jackie Farrell, the Yankee publicity man, as he tells the story.

"No," said Yogi, "but I saw him."

"Did you talk with him?"

"Sure."

"What did he say?"

"Hello, Yogi."

"And what did you say?"

"I said, 'Hello, Pope.'"

This was Yogi Berra, and still is.

All in all, 1959 wasn't a bad year for Yogi, the thirty-four-year-old ballplayer. He could still hit the long ball. His home-run total dipped again, down to 19, but he hammered out 135 hits, 25 for doubles, to finish with a batting average of .284, and he walloped home 69 runs.

For once, however, Casey and the Yankees needed more than Berra's bat for a championship performance. They finished the season in third place and, for only the second time since Yogi had joined the club, out of the World Series.

150

Although 1960 would tell another story, there was no doubt in the minds of baseball that Yogi was in his final stretch as an active big league star. However, there were still a few good hits left in that bat of his.

Chapter 18

In the first weeks of the 1960 season, Casey Stengel put Yogi into left field. Except for the occasional game when he spelled Ellie Howard behind the plate, left field was his position for the year, and it wasn't a bad year for a man who had passed his thirty-fifth birthday.

He played in only 120 games that year, often only in the role of a pinch hitter, but he still collected 99 hits and connected for 15 home runs. There was no doubt about his contribution to the Yankee drive to the league championship, since they put Yogi into the line-up, but the big guns in 1960 were Mickey Mantle and young Roger Maris, who was to write one of the more dramatic stories of baseball in 1961.

The Yanks played the Pittsburgh Pirates for the World Championship, that fall of '60, and it was in a pregame interview that Danny Murtaugh, the Pirates' manager, indicated how much baseball men respected even the "aging" Berra.

"Sure, the Yankees have some big bats in Mantle,

Skowron, and Howard. But the man we'll worry about most is Yogi Berra."

It was Paul Richards, manager of the Chicago White Sox, who said, that year, "Berra is the toughest man in baseball, when the game is up for grabs. He is by far the toughest man in the league in the last three innings."

Danny Murtaugh had as good a scouting outfit as any manager in the league, and the reports he got all verified that lavish statement of Paul Richard's.

"They say he's slipping," said Murtaugh. "I'll have to see it to believe it."

Yogi had one of his better performances in the annual classic. He slammed out 7 hits and added another home run to his World Series total. It wasn't enough to take the championship, however. The Pirates went home with it that year, with the help of Lady Luck.

A double-play ball headed for Tony Kubek, in the seventh and deciding game, but as the fates would have it, the ball took a bad hop on the hard Pittsburgh infield and hit the Yankee shortstop on his throat. Instead of three out and no score, the "lucky break" gave the Pirates a lift, and they hammered the lead run over the plate. The Yankees, still plenty of fight in them, scored in the top of the ninth to tie the score, but a home run by Bill Mazeroski in the bottom of the ninth finished them off.

"That dirty, rocky infield beat us!" raged Yogi, back in the clubhouse, when it was all over. "We didn't lose! They took it away from us!"

The Yankees were going to lose more than the Series in the tail end of 1960. They lost George

Weiss. Or rather, they fired him. They fired him, they said, because he was too old for his job in the front office. George Weiss was sixty-five.

More shocking to the baseball world than the firing of Weiss was the firing of Casey Stengel. Sure, Casey was seventy years old, according to the calendar; but, according to the fans, he was seventy years young.

"And look at his record! Ten pennants in twelve years! You just don't fire a man with a record like that!"

But the owners of the New York Yankees, Dan Topping and Del Webb, were not sentimentalists. They were realists, or so they believed. Even though the Yankees had won the pennant, they reasoned that the team was growing old, that it needed new blood. They were to prove themselves rather devoid not only of sentiment, but of loyalties, with the years to come.

Roy Hamey, who had worked as an assistant to George Weiss, became the general manager of the club. Ralph Houk, who was the back-up catcher for Yogi and had for more than ten years managed in the minors and coached for Casey, was named the new Yankee manager.

As we said, 1961 belonged to Roger Maris. This was the year of years in the battle for the home-run crown, with Maris and Mantle neck and neck for most of the race. Mickey Mantle gave way to injuries; still he finished the season with 128 RBIs and 54 home runs. Roger Maris kept up the hot pace through July, August, and September, with the kind of pressure few people can take and stand up.

Babe Ruth, of legend, had hit 60 home runs in one season, and nobody believed that record could ever be

154

equaled, never mind broken. But Roger Maris, with the season coming quickly into its last days, reached that peak of 60. Then broke through that peak, and Ruth's fantastic record, with his 61st homer, to establish a record.

That feat of Roger Maris overshadowed all other events in the baseball world that year, but one man doesn't make a team, and one man doesn't win the pennants.

It wasn't a bad year for Yogi Berra, either. Again, but sadly for the last time, he collected more than 100 hits for his season's work. This time it was 107, 22 of them for home runs.

On June 6 of that year, in Los Angeles, he banged out the 2,000 hit of his career, and they stopped the game to wheel out a huge cake to celebrate the occasion.

It was in Los Angeles, incidentally, that they got Yogi to play a bit part in the movie comedy, *That Touch of Mink,* starring Cary Grant and Doris Day, no less.

Yogi may no longer have been able to get around the bases as fast as he once did, but he could still power the ball. And he was still good enough a ballplayer to play the outfield almost flawlessly in the World Series as the Yanks whipped the Cincinnati Reds in five games to take the World Championship one more time.

But Berra was getting too far on in years for full-time duty on the diamond, as a catcher or as a fielder. He didn't need to be told, either. In 1962 he reached his thirty-seventh birthday, and for active playing duty in baseball, a thirty-seven-year-old is practically an ancient.

Yogi hit 10 home runs in 1962 but his batting average fell to .224, his lowest average in all the eighteen seasons he went to bat in a Yankee uniform. In all, as outfielder and pinch hitter, he appeared in only eighty-six games in 1962. For the first time in thirteen years, he was not selected to make an appearance in the annual All-Star game. In the World Series against the National League Champions, the Giants, a series won yet once more by the Yankees, he came to bat only twice, as a pinch hitter, going 0 for 2.

"I'd like to play just one more year," he said, after the Series, "if the Yankees want me."

The Yankees wanted him. He was a drawing card. The fans always came in droves just to get a look at Berra take a swing at the ball—maybe blast it into the stands. They hired him as a player-coach for 1963, but this would be his last year as a player for the New York club.

The "old man" of thirty-eight gave the Yankees more than they bargained for in that last season as a player. Before the end of the second week in July, he belted a 3-run homer to beat the Los Angeles Angels, 4–3. It was his 335th lifetime homer that did it. By mid-July he was batting up with the leaders of the League with a .304 average. When he wasn't coaching at first base, he was playing the outfield; even occasionally behind the plate. In all, he appeared in 64 games and closed the season with a respectable batting average of .293.

His last time at bat as a Yankee came in the World Series with the then Los Angeles Dodgers. It was a

Series the Dodgers won in four straight games. Yogi went up to the plate as a pinch hitter, and though he lined the ball hard, he lined it straight at the Los Angeles right fielder.

That was it for Yogi as a Yankee ballplayer, that line drive, his last swing at the ball for the New York ball club. He had played in 2,116 regular-season games for that Yankee organization of stars and super-stars; appeared in more games than any other Yankee in the history of the club with the exception of Iron-Man Lou Gehrig. In addition, he had appeared in 75 World Series games for the Yankees.

His lifetime statistics for the New York club, over a period of eighteen years reads: Batting average—.285; 358 home runs; 1,430 runs batted in. His average in 14 World Series was .274, with 12 for all the bases. He played in 15 All-Star games. He holds pages full of records for his fielding and batting in both regular-season play and World Series play. Here are just a few of them:

No catcher in the game has hit as many home runs as Berra.

He holds the record for the most consecutive chances for a catcher without an error—950; and consecutive games without an error—148.

His 6 double-plays as a catcher tied an American League record, and his 30 home runs in a season (which he did twice) tied another record for catchers.

In World Series competition, he was the first to hit a pinch-hit home run.

He played in more World Series than anyone else—14.

He played in more World Series games than anyone else—75.

The 39 runs he batted in in World Series play has yet to be matched.

It was a great record with which Yogi Berra might have closed the books on a great baseball career, but the book refused to be closed. True enough, Yogi was finished as an active ballplayer for the Yankees, but wheels were turning within wheels in the Yankee front office, and the baseball career of Yogi Berra was far from over. It was going to take a new and a very surprising turn, for almost everyone but Yogi, before the last pages were written on that dramatic baseball season of 1963.

Chapter 19

Immediately after the 1962 World Series, Roy Hamey, the Yankees general manager, decided that 1963 was going to be his last year with the club. His mind was on retirement. He had had about enough of the tensions of his office. He suggested that Ralph Houk take over his job, and Ralph Houk, with a bit of persuasion, agreed to take it. All this bit of maneuvering was very hush, hush, of course. It was strictly a business secret.

The question was: Whom do we get to manage the club on the field?

Dan Topping, president of the Yanks, thought it should be someone who could help bring the fans back to the Yankee Stadium. The Yankees had been winning the championships, but it was the new franchise in the expanded National League, the New York Mets, with Casey Stengel managing the club, that was pulling the crowds, while the attendance at the Yankee games dwindled. It was no trade secret that the main draw of the fumbling and bumbling Mets was the colorful "Old Case" himself. What was important in selecting the new manager for the Yankees, as Topping saw it, was not managerial experience so much as the personality to compete with Stengel's ability to get coverage in the sports columns, as well as the ability to win the loyalty and the support of the fans.

The Yankees didn't have to look far for such a man. He was right there on the payroll. He was Yogi Berra. Berra was easily the most colorful man, with the possible exception of "Old Casey," in baseball. He was certainly the most popular player among the New York fans. And he had demonstrated for a long time how much copy he could draw in the newspaper columns.

Early in the spring training camp of 1963, Ralph Houk went into action. He asked Yogi to meet him at his hotel, from where they both went to join Dan Topping and Roy Hamey on Topping's yacht.

Everything was secret, top secret, and it had to be kept that way for some reason only the top brass can explain.

"How would you like to manage?" Houk asked of Yogi, once the boat was out to sea.

"Manage who?"

"Here. The Yankees," said Houk.

"Where the deuce are you going?" asked Berra.

The answer to that question seemed more important to Yogi than the prospects of managing the championship ball club.

Ralph Houk explained.

There was more talk.

"I don't know," said Yogi. "I'll have to talk to Carmen about it."

Talking with Carmen was all right with Dan Topping, but he wanted Yogi's answer in twenty-four hours. He got it. Yogi Berra was going to be the manager of the New York Yankees in 1964.

The deal, the top brass insisted, had to be kept secret and Yogi, for all his love of talking, managed to keep it secret right through the 1963 season. But baseball players have keen ears, and sportswriters have keener ears. The ballplayers couldn't help hearing Houk and Berra talking on the bench during a game, and the questions they asked each other and the answers they gave each other, all about the different players, strategy, and various other aspects of the game, had them guessing the truth. The newspapermen began their guessing in the press early and in mid-September 1963, Hy Goldberg, one of the nation's top sportswriters writing in the Newark *News,* scooped them all with the correct prediction that Ralph Houk was going to move upstairs in the Yankee organization and that Yogi Berra was going to take over the reins as the manager of the Yankee club.

The announcement of the change in the Yankee line-up became official on October 22, 1963, at a press conference in the Crystal Suite of the Sheraton-Plaza Hotel in New York. It no longer came as a surprise to the baseball world, but it did give the sportswriters their first opportunity to ask Berra a lot of questions about his new job.

Yogi had come into the press conference feeling awkward and out of place, but one look around the room at all the newspapermen and the big smiles on their faces put him at ease. He knew he was among friends, and he became his simple, natural self.

161

"When they first told me about this," he said, the grin all over his face, "I almost flipped."

"How come you only signed for a one-year contract?"

"I want to see if I can manage."

"What do you know about managing a ball club, Yogi?"

"I have observed from watching," said Yogi in his inimitable way of using the English language.

"What do you expect will be your biggest problem, Yogi?"

"If I can manage," came back the new manager, crisply.

"What makes a good manager?" persisted the sportswriters.

"A good ball club," said Yogi, and no manager ever made a more honest statement.

The general reaction to Berra's elevation to the managerial post, especially among baseball men, was good. Almost unanimously they agreed that Yogi would prove a wise choice on the part of the Yankees' top brass.

Hank Greenberg said, "Yogi should make a terrific manager."

Paul Richards, a little more restrained, said, "Berra will make a fine manager."

Al Lopez, more enthusiastic, said, "Berra will be a superb manager."

His old pal, Joe Garagiola, declared, "Yogi is a winner. He always has been a winner. He'll be a winner all the time."

There was no doubt about Yogi Berra's baseball wisdom, but it was Bill Dickey who put his finger on the major problem Yogi would encounter, managing the New York Yankees, discipline.

"He'll be managing men he's played with for years. He was one of them. It's one thing playing with men; it's another thing managing them. The change won't be easy. It all depends on how Berra handles the situation. I hope he makes a go of it."

"Hey, Whitey," called Yogi, when he was coaching the Yankees in 1963, "let's you and me and Mickey go out to eat together tonight." (Whitey Ford and Mickey Mantle were his closest pals on the New York club.)

"Nothing doing," said Whitey to Yogi's invitation. "You can't eat with the fellows any more." Ford was cold. "You're a coach now."

"Officers don't eat with enlisted men," chipped in Mickey Mantle, equally coldly.

"Aw, come on, fellers," begged Yogi. "You don't want to talk that way. I'm still Yog, ain't I?"

They went out to eat together all right, but Berra would find that old fellowship was going to get in his way as the manager and the disciplinarian of the club.

Ballplayer and coach, he was the friendly, easy-going pal to every man on the diamond, visiting team, umpires and all.

"How's the family?"

"Glad you're feeling better."

In the clubhouse, before the game, he walked around in his shirttails, talking to anyone at hand, slapping one man's back, mussing up some other man's hair. A man's character doesn't make hairpin turns. Yogi Berra couldn't help being the friendliest man that ever donned a baseball uniform. It was going to cost him, as the seventeenth manager in the story of the New York club.

He started well enough with the Yankees' Rookie School in Hollywood, Florida, early in February, with Whitey Ford as the pitching coach, Frankie Crosetti as the infield coach, Johnny Neun to show the recruits how to play the infield, and the great Joe DiMaggio in the role of special batting coach.

The rookies were all lined up in centerfield, about fifty of them, and Yogi made his inaugural address as manager of the New York Yankees, an address which surprised not only his coaches, but the sportswriters as well.

"Everybody in bed by midnight," was only one of the regulations Yogi set down, to the double-take of those who heard him lay down the law.

It was don't do this and don't do that, if you want to play ball for the Yankees.

"The greatest thing in baseball is to be a Yankee," he said, "but you've got to bend your back and fight to get there."

He even had the young fellows go through calisthenic drill, something no one remembered the Yanks had done before.

It worked well enough with the youngsters. Yogi didn't know any of them, hadn't slapped their backs or ruffled their hair. It was going to be a bit different with his old pals on the club.

The regular sessions at the preseason training camp got off to a better start than anyone might have expected. Yogi seemed to be in full control, handling the ballplayers with the kind of authority a manager is supposed to possess. But, by the end of the training

164

period the Yankees had lost 15 of their 27 exhibition games and the sportswriters began to notice trouble.

Not Yogi.

"We'll win the pennant," he said. "We've got the best players in the league."

But the pressure was on Yogi Berra. He knew it. Ralph Houk had won three straight pennants for New York. Yogi had to repeat.

"Of course," he said, always bluntly honest, "if we win, they'll say that Mickey Mouse could have managed the club to the pennant. If we lose, they'll say it's my fault."

With that strange prescience he seemed to have, and exhibited before, that odd sense of what was to come in the days ahead, he added, to a rather stunned newsman, "Maybe I'll quit even if we win."

Yogi didn't quit. He wasn't a quitter. But there were more dramatics in that season of 1964 than Yogi might have anticipated, and a climax that no one in the baseball world might have expected.

With a seasoned pitching staff headed by Whitey Ford (who doubled as coach), Jim Bouton, and Al Downing, it was a fair bet that the Yanks would start out winging toward the pennant race with the opening "Star-Spangled Banner." They didn't. Whitey lost the opener. Jim Bouton, who had won 21 games for Ralph Houk, had won only 8, lost 9, when the season was at its halfway mark. The bull pen, Bill Stafford, Steve Hamilton, and Hal Reniff, was a rest home for sore arms.

There were other "health" problems. Tony Kubek, Roger Maris, and Tommy Tresh all suffered one kind of an injury or another. There were days and weeks when Yogi just didn't have a complete line-up of his regulars in the field. Yet Yogi never lost his cool. He made errors in judgment, but those same errors were overcome, by his handling of his players. He was patient with them; did not panic. At the end of May the Yankees were in fifth place in the league standings, 4½ games behind the leading Baltimore Orioles.

Doubts about the wisdom of the Yankees' choice of Berra to manage the New York club became a fairly common item for certain sportswriters. They began to question his decisions.

He pulled his starting pitcher, Rollie Sheldon, out of the game, with New York leading by five runs, for a pinch hitter, who struck out. The relief man, Pete Mikkelsen, was clobbered, and the Yanks lost the lead and the ball game.

He put shortstop Phil Linz in at third, and the great third baseman Clete Boyer at short, which had almost everyone wondering whether Berra hadn't lost all his baseball senses.

Off the field, every sportswriter and a whole lot of fans knew that the Yankees were ignoring the regulations Yogi had set down. Not all of them by any means, but enough to count were hitting the night spots and the bottle as well. And Berra wasn't up to handling the situation. He was too much the "nice guy." He just didn't know how to be tough with his men.

It was Leo Durocher, "The Lip," who said, "Nice guys finish last."

The Yankees weren't going to finish last, but it certainly didn't look like they were going to finish first, either. Still, for all the errors of judgment Berra would be

166

expected to make in this first year of his as a manager, and despite all the shenanigans of his ballplayers off the field, the manager insisted that the club would repeat its triumph of 1963. Perhaps Yogi had another of his famous premonitions, but more likely, he was whistling in the dark, trying to buoy up his own spirits along with the spirits of his players.

But in late August, the Orioles were still leading the league and the Yankees dropped four straight games to the Chicago White Sox to fall 4½ games off the pace. There was no joy among the New York ballplayers as they rode the bus, after that shellacking, to the Chicago O'Hare Airport.

It was on the way to the airport that Yogi finally stepped out of the character he had created and let the fur fly. It was the well-publicized incident on the bus that probably accounted for an abrupt turnabout in both the manager of the Yankees and the men who were supposed to work under his direction.

Phil Linz had bought a harmonica in Chicago. He had bought another for Bobby Richardson. They were going to play hymns from Billy Graham's Hymn Book, according to the Yankee shortstop.

In the bus, Phil, like everyone else, felt the Yanks were no longer in the pennant fight, and like everyone else around him, he felt pretty low about it. He took out his harmonica and, most likely without any disrespect to his manager intended, began to play "Mary Had a Little Lamb."

Yogi, sufficiently irritated with the way things were going on the ball field, whirled around and shouted at Linz, sitting in the rear of the bus, "Shove that thing!"

Linz, sitting next to Joe Pepitone, apparently fed up

167

with everything that was happening with the Yankees, deliberately ignored the manager's orders, and played a Toot-toot on his instrument.

Yogi was on his feet in an instant. For once he demonstrated that he could be as angry with his charges as he was, occasionally, with an umpire on the playing field.

He started for his young ballplayer, and Linz, reading the blood in his eyes, offered the harmonica, apparently in surrender (maybe mock surrender) to Yogi.

Yogi, unappeasable at the moment, took a swat at the harmonica. It cut Pepitone's knee.

"I told you to put that thing away!" barked Yogi.

"What did I do?" came back an aroused Linz. "I give you everything I've got on the field. Let me do what I want when I'm off it!"

"I'll take care of you!" Yogi threatened, then marched back to his seat behind the driver of the bus.

The rest of the way to the airport was thick with silence, the kind of silence that comes before a storm.

But the storm never came.

Linz apologized. He was fined $200.

"That's it," said Yogi. "Incident closed."

The Yankees lost the next two games on their schedule and dropped to 6 games off the pace behind the Baltimore Orioles. If anything seemed certain in baseball—a rare occurrence in the game—it was that Yogi Berra was managing the New York club for the first and last time.

It was from this, their lowest ebb in the season, that the Yankees suddenly took off. The pitching staff suddenly began to pitch in the winning style to which the Yankee fans had long been accustomed. A rookie from the Richmond club, Mel Stottlemyre, began to mow down the opposition. Pete Ramos was bought from the Cleveland Indians, and he proved to be a fireman in the bull pen, ready to put out any blaze the opposing team started. The Yankees took 30 out of 41 games and clinched the flag for Berra, as he had predicted they would, and for New York.

In the National League, the St. Louis Cardinals, managed by Johnny Keane, had clinched their division flag with an even more spectacular finish. Trailing the Philadelphia Phillies by 7½ games, with only ten games to play, they hammered their way to the National League flag on the very last day of the season.

It took seven tough games to decide the World Series in 1964 and St. Louis copped the championship. But the real drama of that '64 season was to take place just about twenty-four hours after all the bats and gloves and uniforms had been put away.

It had been no secret in St. Louis that Keane had been scheduled to be fired, but that was before the Cardinals took the pennant and the series. The St. Louis office did make an effort to reverse its initial intentions by offering Keane a new contract, but it was too late. Keane had already written his letter of resignation and he wasn't going to go back on it.

It was different with Yogi Berra. The New York front office fired Yogi and then tried to soften the blow by offering him the job of "nonuniformed field consultant," if he cared to stay on with the Yankees, but he was out as manager.

The hue and cry that went up from the fans, appalled by this cavalier treatment of their favorite ball-player, their star, their idol, didn't help.

"We have to do what's best for the club," said Houk.

The best the front office of the New York club could do was to hire Johnny Keane to manage the Yankees in 1965, in less than three days after they had callously fired, for all purposes, the man who had served them so well.

The Yankees would pay for this piece of crass business, at the turnstiles, where it hurt.

As for Yogi, there was no taking away from him the glory that comes to a man who leads a major league team to a championship.

He would no longer be a Yankee, and that undoubtedly hurt, but his glorious baseball days were far from over. He was still to write a few pages in the fabulous history of the game.

•

Chapter 20

Joe Garagiola, Yogi Berra's lifetime pal, said of him, "Nothing bad ever happens to Yogi. He is one of God's children."

Still, though he was a thorough gentleman about the affair and never uttered a single word against Ralph Houk, Dan Topping, or any of the other Yankees—players or brass—Yogi had suffered a severe shock. Like every man who is honest at heart, he believed everyone else around him was honest. Like every man with a deep sense of loyalty, he believed everyone else around him was equally loyal. With the ugly developments that followed the 1964 World Series, his firing and the immediate hiring of Johnny Keane by the New York club, he was shocked into the realization that he had been laboring under a serious misconception of the world in which he lived.

Certainly he had made enough errors in his brief managerial stint with the Yankees, but that was to be expected of a "rookie" manager. Besides, he had brought home the American League pennant. A man isn't fired for winning the pennant. The quick hiring of

Johnny Keane was even less palatable to the sensitive Yogi. The haste with which it was done indicated there had been some backroom dealings, and that even while Yogi was taking the Yankees to the top, the front office had secretly been maneuvering to drop him.

For Yogi, this was a crass display of disloyalty and dishonesty. While he held his tongue about it, his faith in men, his faith in those who were supposed to be his friends, must have been severely shaken.

The shock might very well have taken the Yogi out of baseball forever. Fortunately for the baseball world, and particularly the New York Mets, it didn't.

While the fans and the sportswriters were still venting their wrath, verbally, on the New York Yankees' front office for their cold-blooded treatment of Berra, Yogi got a call from Donald Grant, chairman of the board of the New York National League club.

"How would you like to be a coach with the Mets? Maybe you could double as a pinch hitter. How would you like to team up with Casey Stengel again?"

Stengel was good bait. Yogi knew how "Old Casey" felt about him, and he loved the old man. There was something of a father-son relationship between them.

"We can't promise you that you'll step into his shoes, when Case retires," said Grant, "but we certainly will consider it, when he does retire."

"What does Casey think about it?" asked Yogi.

He didn't want Stengel to think that he would be moving into his managerial territory.

"Casey thinks it would be great," came back the Met chairman of the board.

"Let me talk it over with Carmen," said Yogi.

172

He always talked over these decisions with his wife.

Carmen, who knew how much baseball meant to her husband, wasn't going to stand in the way.

Yogi Berra became a coach, and pinch hitter with the New York Mets on November 17, 1964.

The New York Mets had been a lovable but ineffectual ball club in 1964, winning 53 games and losing 109. They had been a lovable and ineffectual club since their very beginning as an expansion ball team in 1962.

George Weiss, who had been fired by the Yankees after serving them so brilliantly in their front office for so many years, was the president of the New York Metropolitan Baseball Club. Casey Stengel, who had been fired from the Yanks, after leading them to ten American League Championships, was its manager. They were both top men in their fields, but building a new team for major league ball is a slow matter, and building a team that will be a contender for the flag a slower matter. It requires a bit more than a little patience on the part of the front office and a tremendous amount of patience on the part of the fans. Happily, both fans and front office possessed an inordinate amount of this patience and even more of that valuable asset, loyalty.

In the beginning, the Mets recruited some great old players. There was home-run slugging Frank Thomas who had played fourteen years for Milwaukee. There was the great ex-Dodger, Gil Hodges. "Vinegar Bend" Mizell of pitching fame came to the Mets, as did Clem Labine, the one-time great relief pitcher for the Dodger organization. So did that one-time batting

173

champion and all-time star of the Cubs and Phillies, Richie Ashburn.

They had all seen glorious service on the baseball fields of various good teams, but their prime years were gone. They were old men as far as the game was concerned. Roy McMillan, a one-time great shortstop was another of these famous "old men" to play with the Mets, and there were many others, including Jim Marshall of the Giants and Gus Bell from Cincinnati.

At the other end of the spectrum of players, there were any number of youngsters out of the minors, most if not all of them without the stuff that makes for a major leaguer. There were "Choo-Choo" Coleman and Joe Ginsberg, "Hot-Rod" Rod Kanehl (whom Casey considered something of a good luck charm) and, of course, there was "Marvelous" Marv Thronberry. They may not have been among the best players who ever decorated a diamond, but they certainly were among the most colorful, and the Met fans loved them.

The Met fans, themselves, were a special breed.

"Let's go, Mets!"

This was the cry that went out at the first sign of a Met rally.

Two out in the ninth, and ten runs behind, if the third man to bat in that final frame so much as got a walk to first base, the park would suddenly become alive with a hoot and a holler of that world-famous shout:

"Let's go, Mets!"

The old Brooklyn fans, who never forgave the

Dodgers for moving to Los Angeles, became Met fans, and rabid fans.

The old New York Giants fans, who were so angered by the Giants' move to San Francisco, became Met fans, and equally rabid.

Fans of Yogi Berra, damning the Yankees for their cavalier treatment of their idol, joined the trend, deserted the Yanks for the Mets.

The American tradition that calls for rooting for the underdog also helped swell the numbers of ardent Met fans. It would be difficult to dig up a team that was more of an underdog than the New York Mets in its first years, nor a fandom more numerous and more loyal for a consistent loser.

Casey Stengel's presence on the club didn't hurt, either. With Yogi Berra as coach, the roster would seem to be complete. Top banana, as they say in show business, second banana, and a complete cast of flamboyant actors.

But it was not going to be burlesque and comedy with the Mets forever. Better, and even glorious times were waiting for them in the wings, to the sheer joy, the ecstasy, that even the most loyal of Mets fans never dreamed he would experience.

For Yogi, of course, baseball was never comedy. It was always a serious business, the core of his life.

He went to bat nine times for the Mets early in his first year with them, 1965, and got two hits. But it was obvious to all, Yogi as well, that his playing days were over.

"It's hard coming back after a whole year layoff," he said. "And my eyes ain't as good as they used to be."

He devoted himself to full-time coaching. He pitched batting practice, passed on his knowledge of hitting to his batters, coached at first base, and lent his experience of so many years to whatever managerial decision had to be made.

"Meet my assistant, Mr. Berra," was the way Casey introduced him to friends and strangers alike.

The hustling, bustling, dramatic action of the ballplayer was now history. In its place was a self-effacing, loyal man who worked around the batting cage, shouted encouragement to his boys from his coaching box just outside the first-base foul line, who quietly talked with his pitchers about the weakness of the different hitters before a game, during the game, and after. None of this was obvious to the fans, but the sportswriters were aware of all his contributions to the Mets; and the Met owners were impressed by the low key in which he deported himself on and off the field (which was most unusual for a man who had achieved such stardom). And perhaps they were even more appreciative of the unstinting quality of loyalty that was so intrinsic to the very nature of Yogi Berra.

Still, when Casey fell and broke his hip at West Point late in the season of 1965, it was not Yogi that the Met top brass put in charge of the club. It was Wes Westrum, another of the coaches of the Mets at the time, who was given the job.

When Stengel retired at the beginning of the 1966 season, it was Westrum who was signed as the club's manager.

In 1967, when Westrum was fired, in late September, Yogi Berra was bypassed again, and another coach, Salty Parker, took the helm to finish the season's play.

Yogi may have been seriously considered by the top brass for the 1968 schedule, but again it was someone else the front office got the managerial spot. This time it was Gil Hodges who got the post.

Yogi, after his fashion, made no comment on these three separate appointments, each of which might very readily have gone to him. There was no doubt that he yearned to manage a major league club again, if only to show the baseball world, and particularly the New York Yankees, that the pennant he had won for the New York American League club had not been just a lucky accident. Still, in that low key he had developed he said nothing and went about his business of coaching in the same loyal way he had so consistently demonstrated. His performance as coach and as man did not escape the notice of either the press or the front office. Eventually he would reap the rewards for it.

Chapter 21

Gil Hodges, who started his baseball career as a catcher and ended as a first-baseman, had wound up a 2,006-game career with the Brooklyn Dodgers with a career batting average of .273. He had hit 370 home runs, 14 of them with the bases loaded, and batted in 1,274 runs. He had played in seven World Series and in eight All-Star games. He walloped 9 home runs as a Met in 1962, its first year as a major league club, and batted in 17 runs before his knees gave way and his career as an active player came to an end.

He then went to Washington, where he managed the Senators for five seasons, and almost had them in contention for the pennant for once.

He was always strictly business, and he was a tough disciplinarian.

They tell of the time he walked into the clubhouse, in Washington, and made a little speech to his "boys." He had been witness to four of them breaking the curfew he had set, and Hodges wasn't going to let anyone in his squad flaunt any of the rules he had set for them.

"Some of you," he said, "have broken curfew. If you want to pay your $50 fine right now, the case will be closed. If the money isn't in by the end of the day, we'll have another meeting, I'll name names, and the fines will go up to $100. You can leave your checks on my desk."

It wasn't more than half an hour later that Joe Pignatano, one of his coaches who was later to join him with the Mets, came to him with a sheaf of checks, and a big grin all over his face.

"That was a pretty smart move," he told his boss, Gil Hodges. "You gave four fellows a chance to admit they broke curfew. So far, seven guys have already dropped their $50 checks."

Hodges managed the Mets to 73 wins in 1968, the highest total season victories they had been able to garner in their seven-year history. The big story for the club, for Gil and for New York, however, was to be 1969. Nineteen sixty-nine was the year of destiny for the most colorful baseball team that ever played in the New York Metropolitan area.

It was a young team in 1969. There were only two players who were with the original 1962 Mets. One of them was Ed Kranepool, the hard-hitting youngster who had come straight to the New York club from James Monroe High School in the Bronx. The other was little Al Jackson, who pitched only 11 innings in that glorious 1969 campaign.

Ken Boswell was a twenty-two-year-old youngster out of Austin, Texas, with just about three years of professional ball behind him.

Cleon Jones had scored 26 touchdowns in high school football, and 17 TD's in two seasons of foot-

179

ball at Alabama A & M, when the Mets picked him up.

Ron Swoboda had played state championship basketball, and had been the goalie and captain of his high school soccer team.

Jerry Koosman, who hailed from Appleton, Minnesota, had pitched only for the Army team at Fort Bliss before he became a Met.

Gary Gentry was plucked out of Arizona State University.

Tom Seaver was one of the nation's leading collegiate pitchers at the University of Southern California. The Atlanta Braves signed him to what the Commissioner of Baseball ruled an illegal contract. When Seaver was told by the top office he was free to sign with any club in either league, except the Atlanta Braves, he joined the Mets and received a bonus of $51,500.

Tug McGraw became a Met before he had hurled a single pitch in a professional game.

Buddy Harrelson, that star shortstop, was a Met in 1969. So was the slugging Wayne Garrett.

Jerry Grote had been signed out of the Astro farm club in Oklahoma City after the Houston club had, for all purposes, discarded him.

Tommy Agee came from the White Sox, the thirty-one-year-old Don Cardwell from St. Louis, Ed Charles from Kansas City, Al Weis from the Chicago White Sox, and Donn Clendenon, with his potent bat, was lured out of retirement, his studies in law, and his duties as vice-president of the Scripto organization to join the New York club.

With its mixture of age and youth in rather good

proportion, Gil Hodges had a promising squad in hand, the beginning of 1969. No one could guess, however, how promising.

Hodges said the Mets would win 85 games in 1969. That was 12 games more than they had won in 1968, and no one took Gil very seriously.

The Las Vegas price on the Mets was 100–1, the same price they had carried the year before, and no one was placing any bets on the New York club, even at those odds.

And in April of the new season, the Mets did nothing to prove Hodges right and Las Vegas wrong. They lost 4 of the first 6 games. They were 9 and 11 at the end of April. By the end of May they were 9 games off the pace of the leading Chicago Cubs, with only 21 victories to their credit.

In the last days of May, however, the Mets suddenly erupted and went on to win 11 straight games. By the end of June they were in second place. New York fans began to get excited. All at once, the club that had been in the cellar, or just next door to it, for all of its existence was way up there in the fight for the pennant. Unbelievable? Perhaps. But true!

At the end of August the Mets were still in there, but 5 games behind Chicago.

On September 10 it happened. The New York Mets had caught up and passed the embattled Cubs. It was New York that was in first place, and it was there to stay for a hysterical New York and the maddest bunch of fans to root a team to victory.

There were more miracles for the Mets in 1969.

They beat the Atlanta Braves, Champions of the Western Division of the National League, in three straight games, to take the National League Championship. Then, after suffering a defeat in the first game of the World Series, they whipped the Baltimore Orioles, champions of the American League, in four straight, to take the World Championship.

Who would have believed it?

The faith of Mrs. Joan Whitney Payson, the owner of the Mets, the brilliant managing of Gil Hodges, the grit of his ball club, the fanaticism of the fans, all must be counted when it comes to listing those responsible for what was called, and is still called, the Miracle of 1969.

Joe DiMaggio, who had thrown out the first ball said, "I never saw anything like it."

Tom Seaver, who was always elegant in his phrasing of the English language, declared, "It was the greatest collective victory by any team in sport."

"We're Number One in the world," said the veteran Ed Charles, "and you can't get any bigger than that."

Casey Stengel said, "Amazing!"

Yes, they were the Amazing Mets!

"I never saw any team play the way this team played," said Yogi Berra, delighted to be with a winner once more.

"It was a colossal thing," said manager Gil Hodges.

In 1970 and 1971, the Amazing Mets played good ball, but not good enough to repeat their great triumph of '69.

In 1972 Gil Hodges was dead.

Fate, once more, would call on Yogi Berra to move out of the shadows of his first-base coaching box, to take center stage, and to throw the baseball spotlight on the veteran from the Hill.

Chapter 22

Rube Walker, Eddie Yost, Joe Pignatano, and Gil Hodges were walking off the golf course, after shooting 18 holes. They had begun to walk back to the Ramada Inn in West Palm Beach, where they were staying, to shower and dress for dinner. Suddenly, Gil Hodges collapsed, fell to the sidewalk, and, according to all medical reports, was dead before his head could hit the concrete.

Gil had suffered a heart attack at the end of the 1968 baseball season, but had recovered completely. He had been able to take the tensions of the next three years, and particularly the supertensions of the 1969 miracle, with no signs of discomfort or ailment. This time, on April 2, 1972, with the preseason camp just under way, the attack, coming with no warning at all, ended forever the brilliant career of one of the most respected and honored men who ever played the game.

The day of Hodges' funeral, Donald Grant, the Mets' chairman of the board, and Bob Scheffing, general manager of the Mets, called a press conference at Shea Stadium to announce that the New York National League club had a new manager: Yogi Berra.

Carmen, Yogi's wife, had almost begged her husband not to take on the assignment.

"You've got a good job. Why do you want to take on that headache?"

Joe Garagiola, Yogi's good pal, was more vehement.

"You'd be a fool to take it! You've got the best job in baseball. Today you're a manager, tomorrow you're not. You could be coach of the Mets forever. Don't take it, Yogi."

But Berra was not to be moved. He had wanted that job offered him for a long time, longer than anyone had suspected.

"I wish Gil Hodges were still here, managing the club. But he isn't. And I want to show them I can do it."

The 1972 team Yogi managed was, if anything a stronger team than the World Champions of 1969. Jim Fregosi had been acquired from the Los Angeles Angels and promised to strengthen the infield at third base Jon Matlack, a rookie in 1971, promised to add to the strength of the Met pitching staff. Don Hahn, who had come from Montreal, and Jim Beauchamp from St. Louis, were expected to help with their big bats.

There were two other names to join the Mets in 1972. One of the stars was Rusty Staub, the power hitter, the man who had been the darling of the Montreal Expos, the man they called "Le Grande Orange."

The other was the most fabulous favorite of them all, the all-time great Willie Mays.

Mays had always been popular in New York from the day he donned the uniform of the then New York Giants. His famous basket catches, his great bat, had made him a legend, a folk hero. Legends and heroes, however, don't make a manager's life particularly easy. On the contrary, Yogi was faced with a particularly knotty problem from the moment in May when Willie reported to the club for the first time.

Willie was forty-two years old in 1972, long past his great prime. He could no longer get to the fast ball. His arm was no longer as strong as the arms of the younger men with the Mets, and the balls he once could catch in the outfield with comparative ease, fell for singles, doubles, triples, before his aging legs could reach them. The purchase of Willie Mays by the Met's owner, Mrs. Joan Payson, was a sentimental gesture; not a particularly wise baseball move.

Still, it was Willie Mays, with a home run, who won the very first game he played for the New York club, and Yogi had the constant chant of "We want Willie! We want Willie!" in his ears, every time he left the old slugger out of the Met line up.

Actually, Willie played when he wanted to play, for the most part, sat where he wanted to sit in the dugout, and said what he wanted to say whenever it pleased him to say it. And Yogi could do nothing about it. After all, Willie was the New York idol. What was more important was that Willie was on his squad only because the big boss, Mrs. Payson, wanted him there.

Nevertheless, whatever the difficulties Willie Mays presented to Berra, he was doing all right with his club. By June 1, the Mets had won 30 while losing only 11 and with an average of .732, were leading the league by 5 full games.

The top brass couldn't have been more pleased than Yogi. He was showing the baseball world that the pennant he had won for the Yankees in 1964 was not a fluke performance. He was showing the baseball world that he could manage a major league baseball team to the top.

That was June 1, 1972.

On June 3, George Stone, pitching for the Atlanta Braves, hit Rusty Staub on his right hand, breaking a small bone near the wrist. For all purposes, that was the end of Rusty's bat for the year.

On June 9, Jim Fregosi injured his shoulder. Later he injured his leg. Fregosi was out.

June 16, Cleon Jones was put out of action by an injured elbow.

Buddy Harrelson suffered back trouble. Gary Gentry, who had pitched the Mets to 12 victories in 1971, developed shoulder trouble. Tommy Agee hurt his ribs. Jerry Grote was side-lined much of the time because of bone chips discovered in his elbow.

By the middle of July the Mets had slipped to 5 games off the pace. They were 14 games behind the division leaders by September 1. They wound up the season with a flourish, taking four straight from the Montreal Expos, but they finished the race in third place, 13½ games behind the pace setters.

For once, it seemed that Lady Luck had frowned on the boy from the Hill. But he still had a year to go on the two-year contract he had signed for the Met top brass, and the Met top brass could not fault him for the plague of injuries that had dropped the club out of contention, out of what had looked, in the beginning, like another pennant for New York. They didn't. Yogi would manage the Mets in 1973, and 1973 was going to be quite a year!

Nor was 1972 all that bad for Yogi Berra. On the contrary, 1972 proved to be one of Yogi's greatest, most memorable years in the game.

On January 18, 1972, eight men were informed that they had been elected to receive baseball's greatest honor: election to the Hall of Fame. Among those names were the great left-hand hurler Vernon Louis ("Lefty") Gomez; the pitcher who had toiled so magnificently for the Dodgers, Sanford ("Sandy") Koufax; Joshua ("Josh") Gibson, who had walloped close to 800 home runs, playing for such black teams as the Homestead Grays and the Pittsburgh Crawfords, as well as Latin-American nines; Walter Fenner ("Buck") Leonard, another black star with black baseball clubs; Early ("Gus") Wynn who had hurled 300 victories for Washington, Cleveland, and Chicago; William Harridge who had been president of the American League and chairman of the board until the day of his death; and Lawrence Peter ("Yogi") Berra.

It was Yogi who was named first, simply because he was first in the alphabetical order of the men honored for their long and exceptional contribution to the game. It was Yogi who, for the same reason, was the first to receive the award, and make the first speech at the impressive rituals in Cooperstown, New

York, the residence of the Baseball Hall of Fame and Museum.

Yogi had a speech all ready. Carmen had written it for him.

"I have to put on my glasses," he said, as he reached for the speech in his pocket.

"I guess the first thing I ought to say," he added, before reading the speech Carmen had prepared, "is that I thank everybody for making this day necessary."

He was kidding, getting the laugh on himself, recalling that speech he made so long ago in St. Louis, when the people from the Hill collected all that money to buy him a new car.

Everyone laughed. Not at Yogi. With him.

Then he read his speech.

It was simple and it was honest, and completely characteristic of the man.

"I want to thank Bill Dickey," he said, "for polishing me up as a catcher. I want to thank George Weiss for giving me my first New York contract. I want to thank my wife, Carmen, the perfect baseball wife."

He went on, thanking the men who had helped him fashion his career, then, more quietly, "My only regrets are that my parents are not here to enjoy this moment with me, that my brother John is not here, and that Gil Hodges is not here. I hope they are proud of me today."

Joe Garagiola, Yogi's pal, was at the celebration, and he was seen to wipe a tear from his eyes. There were other wet eyes at the celebration, as Yogi's voice cracked, and then a reverent stillness.

"I want to thank baseball," Yogi said at last. "It has given me more than I hoped for. When I am finished, I hope I have given it something back."

Yogi had already given much to the game. He would give still more in the years ahead.

Chapter 23

"What's wrong with the Mets?"

That's what the fans were asking, as Yogi Berra's club just couldn't get started in the 1973 pennant fight.

The trouble came early and in large doses. Rusty Staub was hit in the hand again, this time his left hand. Buddy Harrelson was hurt. So were Cleon Jones, John Milner, and Jerry Grote. Jon Matlack couldn't get out of the way and had his skull fractured by a line drive. Willie Mays was hurting.

By mid-July, the Mets were in last place in the Eastern Division of the National League, 10 full games off the pace.

Yogi, for the first time anyone could remember, began to hear the "boos" of the Met faithful every time he walked out onto the field, to talk to a pitcher or to take him out of the game.

Donald Grant, chairman of the board, was beleaguered by the sportswriters.

"What are you going to do about Berra? He isn't doing much for the Mets."

There were some who didn't hesitate to write that Grant had made an error, hiring Yogi as manager in the first place.

And Grant didn't help.

"We have no intention of dropping Berra as the Met manager," said the club chairman of the board. "You can't blame him for all the injuries the team has suffered."

And that would have been a fine statement for Yogi, if Grant had stopped there. He didn't.

"No," he repeated, "we have no intention of firing Berra *unless the public demands it.*"

The public had begun to demand it. Grant knew that well enough. With the chairman's statement to the effect that the front office was willing enough to let Yogi go, the clamor of the fans for Berra's scalp took on a bit of steam.

Strangely enough, however, there was a considerably larger body of fans who stuck to their support of the beleaguered manager of the Mets. They liked Yogi, they knew that no one man could be held responsible for the poor showing of their club, and they demonstrated their loyalty to the manager in typical Met fan fashion.

The New York *Post,* falling in line with the hue and cry of "What's wrong with the Mets?" conducted a poll of its readers.

"Who is to blame? M. Donald Grant, chairman of the board; Bob Scheffing, general manager; Yogi Berra, manager; all of them; none of them?

It was Scheffing who led the balloting with 1,448 votes. Grant was next with 1,207 votes. Only 611, less than 10 per cent of the fans, put the onus for the team's miserable showing on Yogi Berra.

Berra took the boos, the innumerable sports columns that questioned his abilities, as well as the spineless remarks from the front office, in stride. He was a ballplayer's ballplayer. There was no one in the game who knew baseball better than Yogi. With almost half his regulars on the hospital list, and with Tug McGraw, the ace relief pitcher, giving up an average of almost 5 runs a game, there was no way that the Mets could be like anything approaching a pennant contender.

Still, on August 15, 1973, with the Mets still in the cellar and 7½ games behind the league leaders, the St. Louis Cards, Yogi calmly and deliberately announced that the New York club was not out of the race.

"There's lots of time yet," he said. "We can still do it."

And he wasn't making noises in the dark, so that he wouldn't be afraid to walk past a cemetery.

"Look at all the other clubs on top," he said. "They're stumbling and fumbling around like they don't want to win. All we have to do is put a few good games together."

He was an astute observer and his predictions were generally made on sound ground and with good logic.

"Everybody in the division has had some kind of winning streak, except us. We're due for one. And when we do, just watch us go."

August 22, Tug McGraw made his forty-second appearance on the mound as a relief pitcher. August 22, Tug McGraw won his first game of the season.

Everything and anything is possible in baseball, and the Met fans seized on McGraw's win as a happy omen. Maybe the streak Yogi had predicted had begun.

But the Mets lost the next 3 out of 4. On August 27, the Amazings were still 12 games under the .500 mark. They had climbed out of the cellar, ½ game ahead of Philadelphia but still far behind leading St. Louis, and only 33 games left to play in the season.

It looked hopeless, but Yogi Berra insisted, "We can still do it." Yogi did not panic. Instead, he was more relaxed, more patient with his players. Waiting, scheming, planning.

And suddenly the Mets, if not the fans, began to believe it.

Rusty Staub hit a grand-slam home run to sweep the series with the Padres. Tug McGraw got saves 14 and 15, and Koosman, with an assist by Buzz Capra, pitched a shutout. The Mets had gained 2 full games on the Cards and were only 5½ games behind.

A 5½-game lead is a mighty big lead to overcome with less than 30 games left in the schedule, but the excited Jerry Koosman shouted, in the clubhouse, after his victory, "It's beginning to feel like 1969!"

"If the pitching keeps up," said Jerry Grote.

"That's what I've been telling you," said Yogi Berra, sensing the growing excitement among his ballplayers. "We can do it!"

More excited than all of them, however, was young, ebullient Tug McGraw.

"We're going to be the first team that was last in August to win the pennant!"

Then, almost as if he had had a sudden vision,

"You've gotta bee-lieve!" he cried. "You've gotta beeee-lieve!"

That cry, "You've gotta bee-lieve!" became the battle cry of the Mets and the Met fans, but not just then.

St. Louis and the New York club split their four-game series. The Mets had climbed out of the cellar, dropped right back into it, and finally out of it for the rest of the season on August 31.

There were still no signs of the streak Yogi had hoped for, and it was the Cards still in first place by 5½ games; and only twenty-three games left in the schedule.

"Seaver, Matlack, Koosman, and Stone, from now on," announced Yogi Berra in the clubhouse, "go on a four-day rotation. The Cards are going nowhere, and we've got a shot [at the flag] now. We've got to take it."

September 10. The Mets had climbed into fourth place in the Eastern Division standings, ahead of Chicago, and only 3 games behind St. Louis. Pittsburgh was ½ game behind the leaders; Montreal, 2½.

Abruptly there were signs of pennant fever in the greater metropolitan area of New York.

St. Louis slipped to third place, 2 games off the pace, with the Pittsburgh Pirates in the lead. Montreal was now ½ game out of first. As for the Mets, there were only 2½ games separating them from the Pirates, and a five-game "crucial series" between them next on the schedule.

Pennant fever in New York began to grow.

The Mets were clobbered by Pittsburgh in the first

of that set-to, and Pittsburgh figured that the race was all over and the championship theirs.

They didn't reckon on the "impossible."

In the next game, 3 runs behind in the ninth, the Amazing Mets rallied for 5 runs, held off the Pirates' counterattack in their half of the ninth, to beat them 6–4.

"You've gotta bee-lieve!"

Back in Shea Stadium, where the "crucial series" continued, Tug McGraw came out of the bull pen to stop a Pirate threat, and the Mets won again, easily, 7–3.

Next! The Pirates were leading 2–1 in the eighth inning. The Mets tied the score. The Pirates scored a run in the ninth. The Mets matched it. In the thirteenth, with Richie Zisk on first base, Dave Augustine hit what looked like a 2-run homer off Ray Sadecki; the ball hit the top of the fence, bounced into the glove of an amazed Cleon Jones; Jones whirled and threw to Garrett; Garrett flipped the ball to young Ron Hodges; Hodges made the tag, and, unbelievably, Zisk was out at the plate.

"You've gotta beee-lieve!"

The Mets, alive, scored in their half of the thirteenth. Three in a row over the leading Pittsburgh Pirates.

"Yes, sir! You've gotta beee-lieve!"

Seaver, "Tom Terrific," pitched the fifth game of that big series, a 5-hitter, while the Mets walloped the Pirate pitching for 10 big runs.

With only nine days left in the schedule, with a record of 77 games won and 77 games lost, a .500 average, Yogi Berra and his Amazing Mets were in first place.

"You certainly have got to beee-lieve!"

The Mets had climbed out of the cellar which they had occupied until the very end of August. They were in first place to stay.

Yogi maneuvered a very tired pitching staff brilliantly, and his boys took 5 of the last 7 games on the schedule to take the Eastern Division of the National League title. The National League Championship was next. That, next to the World Series, was the only championship that really counted.

There were four days of rest for the Mets before they were to meet the Cincinnati Reds for the league pennant, and the Reds had won the Western Division flag with comparative ease, clinched it with still a week to go in the schedule. Even with the four days rest, Yogi realized his boys would be at a disadvantage.

Yogi and Rube Walker watched Seaver, their nineteen-game winner, work out at Shea Stadium, and decided that the star hurler would pitch the opener of the series in Cincinnati.

"You've got to win or lose with your best," said Yogi.

Tom Seaver pitched a beautiful game. He set a league record with 13 strike-outs. He was also responsible for the only run the Mets scored in the game, doubling Harrelson across the plate.

But Jack Billingham, another nineteen-game winner, was even better that afternoon, for the Reds, limiting the Met bats to 2 hits in eight innings.

In the eighth inning, Seaver served a home-run ball

to Pete Rose. In the ninth, Johnny Bench drove one out of the park for Cincinnati's second run, and the ball game.

In the second game of the series, Jon Matlack pitched a 2-hitter to even matters between the two clubs. The teams packed up their bags and traveled to Shea Stadium, where the Mets started from where they had left off and clobbered the Reds by the score of 9–2. It was in this third game that the fiery Pete Rose, trying to break up a double play, spilled the considerably smaller Buddy Harrelson and, responsible or not, started what amounted to a small war between the Red outfielder and the fans.

Rose and Harrelson had taken a couple of swings at each other, in the excitement of the game, but neither was thrown off the field for it. The fans, however, set up a howl and worse, began to throw stuff at the Cincinnati outfielder. It took the pleadings of the Met ballplayers, the warnings of the umpires, and fully fifteen minutes before the halted game could get under way again.

In the fourth game of the series, it was Cincinnati on top again, with Pete Rose hitting one for all the bases and the ball game in the twelfth inning.

It had to be Seaver again for the final game, the game that would decide the National League championship.

Yogi didn't hesitate.

"You've got to win or lose with your best."

And Seaver made his manager proud. He pitched eight and a third innings, giving up 7 hits, while his teammates found the range on Billingham this time and hammered home 7 runs.

Tug McGraw came in to get the last two outs of the game, and the fans came pouring out of the stands in a riotous celebration of the Met victory.

For the second time in their short history, the Mets had won the National League Crown, and this time with Yogi Berra guiding their destiny.

"NOW YOU'VE GOTTA BELIEVE IN MIRACLES"
"METS TELL YOGI THEY BELIEVE VIA 3-YEAR CONTRACT"

The headlines told the story.

"At long last," wrote one sportswriter, "the real Yogi Berra stood up yesterday for all the baseball world to see."

Yogi Berra, Casey Stengel's "My assistant, Mr. Berra," the kid from the Hill had accomplished what no other man, with the exception of Joe McCarthy, had accomplished in the history of baseball. In just three years as a manager, one with the New York Yankees, two with the New York Mets, he had guided a major league club to a pennant in the two different leagues, the American and the National. If ever a man could stand up and do a little crowing, now was the time for Yogi to do it. He didn't.

Joe Garagiola wasn't so modest about his self-effacing, life-long friend.

"He took the job," said Joe, "because he wanted to prove he could manage a major league club. And, by God, he proved it. He can manage. He can manage!"

The World Series with Oakland proved to be anticlimactic. The excitement had all come in that last month of the spectacular race for the pennant, and in the play-offs for the National League pennant.

The Mets were a very, very tired ball club, physically and emotionally spent. Their performance in the battle for the World Championship was, nevertheless, spectacular, and they came within an ace of winning it.

Seaver had pitched the last game in the struggle for the National League flag, and it was Jon Matlack who hurled the opening game, and who should have won it. Errors by the usually reliable Felix Millan and the aging Willie Mays allowed the Oakland club to score 2 runs to defeat the Mets, 2–1.

The Mets took the second game in twelve innings, 10–7.

Oakland took the third set-to, despite Seaver's 12 strike-outs, in the eleventh inning. Score: 3–2.

The fourth game went to the Mets, Matlack and Sadecki holding the California team to 1 run, as the Mets scored 6.

In the fifth game, Koosman, with the aid of Tug McGraw, blanked Oakland to make it 3 games to 2 in favor of the New York Club.

One more win and New York would be World Champions again. But all the steam in the club had just about run out. Tom Seaver was beaten 3–1, and Matlack just finally didn't have it in the seventh and deciding game, as the Mets went down to defeat 5–2.

Nothing to be ashamed of, much for which to be proud, the Mets had given a good account of themselves, despite their failure to win the championship of the world.

There was no moaning and no groaning. Just a tired

bunch of fellows packing up and going home for the long winter after a job well done. And Yogi was one of them. He would play golf. He would spend a good deal of time with his family, watch Dale play professional football, and maybe if Tim made the Pirates, Yogi would just as soon sit up in the stands to watch him play.

Chapter 24

The telephone jangled sharply in the small office underneath the massive concrete pilings at Shea Stadium —manager Yogi Berra's office. It was early in the morning; too early for the players to be at the stadium, but Yogi had some drastic changes in mind and had scheduled an early morning meeting with his coaches to be followed by an 11:00 A.M. practice drill for the team. He had a plan that might give the team the added, "shot in the arm," they needed for the last few weeks of the 1975 season. The team was in sorry straits. They had dropped two in a row to the Pirates, and then looked completely demoralized as they lost three straight to Montreal. They were in trouble, and Yogi was desperately trying to pull the sinking team together.

He reached for the phone, cradled it in his arm.

"Yeah, this is Yogi."

"Yogi," said Don Grant, chairman of the Mets. "I'm sorry to tell you this, but we've made an important decision concerning the management of the team. As of this morning, you are relieved of your duties.

We've got another manager. But I can assure you that we will live up to our agreement. We'll have another job for you in the Mets organization. We'll talk about it at a later date."

There was a pungent silence as Yogi sucked in his breath, hard.

"Yeah, Mr. Grant, I got you. Sort of expected this after we dropped those five games in a row. It'll take me a couple of hours, and I'll be cleared out of here. No, no hard feelings, Mr. Grant. I've been with you ten long years. So long."

Yogi sighed, wearily, as he plunked down heavily into the arms of his favorite chair. He slowly bent down and with an effort, untied the laces of his baseball shoes and kicked them free. He loosened the belt around his pants, stood up, and allowed them to drop about his ankles before he kicked them aside. He ran his strong, chunky hands through his hair, shook his head for just a moment, as if a great weight had lifted and then reached into the freezer for a can of beer. Opening it, he slowly sipped the cold brew:

"Gee that tastes good. I feel better already."

He picked up a towel, vigorously toweled his back and shoulders, and cocked his head as he heard the muted sounds of the players entering the clubhouse.

Suddenly the door opened and Eddie Yost, one of Yogi's coaches came through. He walked over to Yogi, shook his hand.

"Skip, I just heard the bad news. I just want to tell you, that . . ."

Yogi cut him off: "That's okay. Let's not have no mourning here. Maybe it's for the best. You know this

202

business of managing. Here today . . . gone tomorrow. But, Eddie, look. Do me a favor."

"Sure, Skip, anything. You know that."

"Tell the guys I'd like to say good-bye to them, before they go out onto the field. I just want a couple of minutes to collect my stuff. Okay?"

Yost closed the door, leaving Yogi alone. Yogi took another sip of the cooling brew, leaned way back in his chair, closed his eyes for a moment, smiled and reflected on his life.

He had a great life. A life filled with thrills, excitement, and happiness until it was overflowing. A life spent in baseball . . . thirty-three years of it with the Yankees and the Mets, and now . . . for the future . . . perhaps back to the Yankees and his pal Billy Martin. That would be great. Back with Martin, Whitey Ford, and Mantle.

He smiled as he thought about the very beginning of all this. How it began in St. Louis, when he was just a kid of fifteen. He and Joey Garagiola trying out with the St. Louis Cardinals. His great joy for Joey, when he came out of Rickey's office with a contract to play ball for the Cards, and a bonus of $500. The bitter pangs of disappointment, when Rickey turned him down.

And then, he remembered how the whole world opened up for him a couple of weeks later when the Yankees gave him a contract to play for one of their farm teams . . . and a bonus of $500. He remembered the great smile on his father's face when he told him about the bonus. He would never forget that.

He leaned back in his easy chair, and in his mind's eye saw himself suiting up for the first time as a

203

member of the New York Yankees and then how, when Joe DiMaggio walked by and shook his hand, he almost burst with pride. And he remembered, too, the first time at bat at Yankee Stadium, and the roar of 40,000 fans as he drove the first pitch out of the Stadium for a home run. That, too, was a day to remember.

He remembered the many days and nights of bitterness when opposing players ran wild on the bases and he could do nothing to prevent it because of his pitiful throwing. He was slow and uncertain, inexperienced, and then they began to call him all kinds of cruel names. And he remembered the kindness of Casey Stengel and Bill Dickey and how Dickey worked with him; taught him everything he knew . . . and slowly, patiently those long agonizing hours of practice paid off, and he became one of the great catchers in modern baseball.

And he remembered those marvelous Yankee greats that he played with—Joe DiMaggio, Tommy Henrich, his roommate Phil Rizzuto, Billy Martin, Whitey Ford, Don Larsen, Vic Raschi, Allie Reynolds, Moose Skowron, Joe Page, Mickey Mantle, Roger Maris, Bobby Brown, Ralph Houk, and many others.

And, finally, he remembered the night he first met Carmen, his lovely wife, in St. Louis in Biggie's restaurant. It had been a wonderful and full life. He had no complaints.

Suddenly, Yogi's reverie was interrupted by a thunderous clap on the door. It was Eddie Yost, again.

"Skip, all the players are out here, waiting for you. They want to talk. Shake your hand, wish you luck."

Yogi moved out of his chair, quickly. He dressed,

combed his hair, straightened his tie, and walked out into the clubhouse area.

"No speeches, fellas. You know I don't like that kind of thing."

He walked around the clubhouse shaking hands with each player, wishing each good luck. After all the good-byes were over, Yogi did answer questions put to him by a corps of sportswriters that had gathered to talk with him.

"I think this club has a great shot for the pennant. A couple of real good games, and with Pittsburgh and the Phillies losing a couple, and the Mets are right in there to the end.

"I've always had great confidence in this team, and I always tried my best, so I know I did all right. My only regret is that although I won two pennants in four tries, I didn't win the World Series. So that's about the only thing that I didn't do in baseball.

"I don't think I'll do anything for the rest of the year but play some golf, and I'm going to play Sunday for the first time during the summer in thirty-three years," he said.

A reporter for the *News* posed this question:

"Yogi, would you do anything differently, if you could do it all over again?"

"No," said Yogi, "I don't think I would. You do the best with what you have. The team still has good pitching, and a lot of clubs would like their pitching. This kid Tate is going to be a real good pitcher.

"I've been in baseball since I was fifteen years old," said Yogi, "and I want to stay in baseball, but I don't want to force myself on anybody. Sure I'll take a coaching job, but I'll have to wait and see. The Mets have said that I can have a job in the organization doing something. Maybe Billy Martin and the Yankees will come up with something."

The days passed quickly for Yogi as he busied himself with television, golf, and other social activities. For almost two weeks he just didn't think about baseball. They were two of the most pleasant, relaxed weeks that Yogi had experienced in more than thirty-five years of warfare on the diamond. For the first time in his adult life there were no baseball responsibilities. He was free from the rigors and tension of the daily struggle to win ball games. Free from the nagging, critical voices of the sportswriters and broadcasters.

He no longer worried about Tom Seaver's arm, Rusty Staub's bad shoulder, Buddy Harrelson's battered knees, Jerry Grote's hitting, and a thousand-and-one other problems that every big league manager had to solve. He was free at last.

Two weeks passed and then Yogi decided to visit with his long-time friend, and former teammate, Yankee manager Billy Martin.

The Yankees had just lost a heartbreaking game to the Chicago White Sox, 7–6 in eleven innings, and Martin was angry.

"I need you around here with me, Yogi. We have a great club. Maybe a championship team with a couple of changes. Will you join me next season?"

"You're not kidding?" said Yogi.

"No, I'm not kidding," snapped Billy.

Yogi grabbed Martin's hand, pumped it vigorously. "You've got yourself a new coach, Billy. Gonna start looking like the old Yankees," shouted Yogi as he and Martin walked out into the night.

On August 20, the sports pages across the nation featured the story. "Yogi Berra, New Yankee Coach."

"I want to thank baseball," said Yogi, accepting his inauguration into the Hall of Fame in 1972. "It has given me more than I ever hoped for. When I am all finished, I hope I have given it something back."

Yogi Berra, Lawrence Peter Berra, has been giving something back to baseball for a very long time. How much more he will give is anybody's guess. One thing is certain, however, whatever he gives, it will be long remembered.

INDEX

210

211

212

213

GENE SCHOOR has been associated with sports and sports person-alities since his high school days in Passaic, New Jersey. After winning a number of amateur boxing championships in New Jersey, Gene received an athletic scholarship at Miami University (Florida) where the boxing team became contenders for the National Championships during the years that Schoor was a member of the team. Gene captured some eighteen regional boxing championships and won his way to the final round of the 1940 Olympics as a welterweight, only to lose his post on the team due to a broken hand.

Mr. Schoor has been a teacher and boxing coach at both the University of Minnesota and City College, New York, and was also a sports commentator on radio stations WINS, WNBC, and WHN. He has produced and directed radio and television pro-grams with Joe DiMaggio and Jack Dempsey. Currently he di-rects his own public relations firm in New York City. The author of forty books, he has written biographies of many well-known sports figures including *Football's Greatest Coach: Vince Lom-bardi*.